OZ CLARKE'S
WINE COMPANION

TUSCANY

GUIDE
MARC MILLON

D0294017

De Agostini Editions

HOW TO USE THIS BOOK

MAPS
For further information on the wine regions see the Fold-out Map.

Each tour in the book has a map to accompany it. These are not detailed road maps; readers are advised to buy such maps to avoid local navigation difficulties.

═══ Motorway (*Autostrada*)

▬▬▬ Major road

······ Minor road

········ Unpaved road (*Strada non asfaltata*)

◆ Wine property

FACT FILES
Each tour has an accompanying Fact File, which lists sources of information on the region, markets and festivals, and where to buy wine. There is also a short listing of hotels and restaurants.

Ⓗ Hotel
Ⓡ Restaurant

To give an indication of prices, we have used a simple rating system.

Ⓛ Inexpensive
ⓁⓁ Moderate
ⓁⓁⓁ Expensive

WINE PRODUCERS
Producers' names in small capitals refer to entries in the A–Z on page 72.

Visiting arrangements
✓ Visitors welcome
⊘ By appointment
✗ No visitors

Wine styles made
🍷 Red
🍷 White
🍷 Rosé

Please note that guidebook information is inevitably subject to change. We suggest that, wherever possible, you telephone in advance to check addresses, opening times, etc.

While every care has been taken in preparing this guide, the publishers cannot accept any liability for any consequence arising from the use of information contained in it.

First published
by De Agostini Editions
Interpark House
7 Down Street
London W1Y 7DS

Distributed in the U.S.
by Stewart, Tabori & Chang,
a division of US Media
Holdings Inc
575 Broadway
New York NY10012

Distributed in Canada
by General Publishing
Company Ltd
30 Lesmill Road, Don Mills
Ontario M3B 2T6

Oz Clarke's Wine Companion:
Tuscany
copyright © 1997 Websters
International Publishers

Fold-out Map
copyright © 1997 Websters
International Publishers
Text copyright © 1997
Oz Clarke
Maps copyright © 1997
Websters International Publishers
Some maps and text have been
adapted from *Oz Clarke's Wine
Atlas* copyright © 1995 Websters
International Publishers

Guide
copyright © 1997 Websters
International Publishers

Created and designed by Websters
International Publishers Ltd
Axe & Bottle Court
70 Newcomen Street
London SE1 1YT

UK ISBN: 1 86212 034 X
A CIP catalogue record for this book is available from the British Library.

US ISBN: 1 86212 038 2
Library of Congress Catalog
Card Number 97–065431

OZ CLARKE
Oz Clarke is one of the world's leading wine experts, with a formidable reputation based on his extensive wine knowledge and accessible, no-nonsense approach. He appears regularly on BBC Television and has won all the major wine-writing awards in the USA and UK. His bestselling titles include *Oz Clarke's Wine Atlas*, *Oz Clarke's Pocket Wine Guide* and the *Microsoft Wine Guide* CD-ROM.

MARC MILLON
Marc Millon has written many books on wine and food, including *The Food Lover's Companion to Italy* and *The Wine Roads of Italy*.

Associate Editorial Director
Fiona Holman
Associate Art Director
Nigel O'Gorman
Editor
Pauline Savage
Art Editor
Christopher Howson
Sub-editor
Gwen Rigby
Editorial Assistant
Emma Richards
Wine Consultant
Phillip Williamson
DTP
Jonathan Harley
Index
Naomi Good
Editorial Director
Claire Harcup
Pictorial Cartography
Keith and Sue Gage,
Contour Designs
Pictorial Map Editor
Wink Lorch
Touring Maps
European Map Graphics

Colour separations by Columbia
Offset, Singapore
Printed in Hong Kong

Photographs:
Front cover Castello di Volpaia is one of Tuscany's highest wine estates.
Page 1 The hilly region of Chianti Classico provides wonderful slopes for vineyards.
Page 3 Sangiovese is Tuscany's great grape variety.

Contents

Introduction by Oz Clarke *4*
Wine at a Glance *6*
Regional Food *10*
Touring Tuscany *12*

◆

◆

Introduction

Tuscany seems a good place to avoid the gritty realities of modern day life. At every turn, you're faced with the kind of storybook scenes that say nothing's changed since the Renaissance. Stately cypress trees still line the way to castles and farmhouses snugly folded into the side of the hills. The hazy silver grey of olive groves contrasts with neatly combed blocks of vines, and above the rugged hill-tops is that hot, still, Tuscan sky. Wasn't it always like this?

Well, no, not in the wine world, which has seen more upheaval and re-thinking in the last 30 years than any other Italian wine region. Chianti has for generations been the one internationally recognized Italian wine. It was already very famous by the 17th century, and in 1716 the Grand Duke of Tuscany drew precise boundaries to the Chianti region since the wine was being shamelessly copied elsewhere in Italy. By the 1960s, Chianti, in its unforgettable straw-covered litre flask, was Italy's wine ambassador to the world – but despite the bargain-priced bonhomie, the wine inside was likely to be insipid and thin. Italian wine was dying on its knees, and the rush to self-destruction was being led by Tuscany.

Tuscany's timeless countryside is epitomized by the rolling hills of Chianti, seen here near Radda in Chianti. Poppies and other wild flowers bring colour to the vineyards in spring.

But there were a few visionaries who realized that Tuscany was in a perfect position to correct this. Chianti did still have some notable properties amid the sea of mediocrity, and there were pinnacles of quality and potential excellence in the vineyards of Carmignano, Montalcino and Montepulciano. And there were stirrings of an entirely new mood, aggressively international in tone and unconstrained by discredited traditions of Tuscan wine. Down near the seashore at Bolgheri, an astonishing Cabernet Sauvignon called Sassicaia was being grown in minute quantities but to world-wide renown. Piero Antinori, nephew of Sassicaia's owner, seized the trend by using classic French methods and grapes to haul Tuscany kicking and screaming to its senses. Outdated wine laws were openly flouted as hordes of others joined Antinori's bandwagon and made Tuscany the vanguard of the Italian wine revolution.

Nowadays, the invasion of international grape varieties like Cabernet Sauvignon and Chardonnay has been followed by an upsurge of pride in all things Tuscan. As inferior clones are replaced in the vineyard, Sangiovese is being recognized as a potentially great grape. Tuscan Cabernet Sauvignon and Chardonnay *can* be some of the greatest made. But Tuscan Sangiovese has no rivals anywhere else in the world. For a people as proud as the Tuscans, being best at something matters.

Oz Clarke

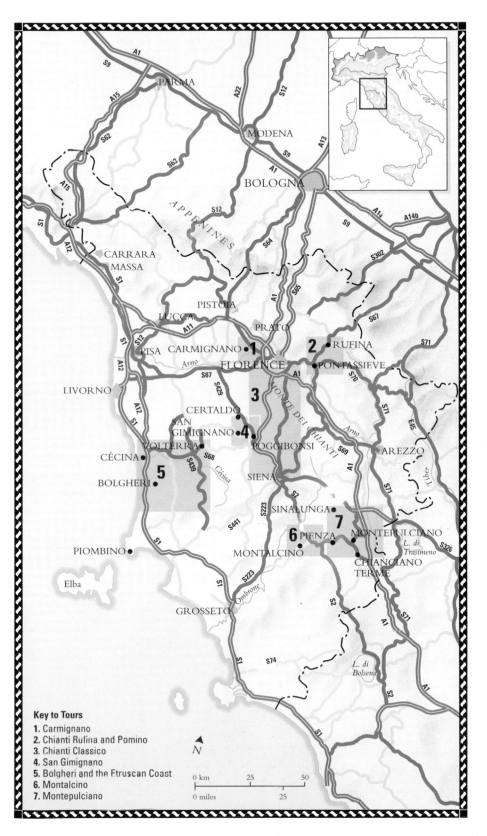

Key to Tours

1. Carmignano
2. Chianti Rufina and Pomino
3. Chianti Classico
4. San Gimignano
5. Bolgheri and the Etruscan Coast
6. Montalcino
7. Montepulciano

N

0 km   25   50

0 miles   25

Wine at a Glance

The Tuscan wine scene can seem complicated at first, with numerous DOC/DOCGs and vini da tavola (see page 7), but nearly all the finest wines come from the seven zones covered in the tours. Much of the best is Sangiovese-based red, but there are other outstanding examples based on Cabernet Sauvignon and other foreign varieties. The whites are mostly neutral and dry but there are increasing numbers of concentrated, characterful examples.

Rosso di Montalcino (left) starts with a deep ruby colour but takes on a mid-garnet hue within five years. Pale Vernaccia di San Gimignano becomes deeper gold in a year or so.

Grape Varieties

In addition to two native varieties – the red Sangiovese and the white Vernaccia – Tuscany has a number of 'international varieties', although only Cabernet Sauvignon and Merlot have met with resounding success.

Sangiovese

Italy's most widely planted grape is the most important variety in Tuscany. Only in high, sloping sites, with reduced yields and improved vinification does Sangiovese reveal its true capabilities. Despite a tendency to high acidity, firm tannins and leanness, this late-ripening variety can be remarkably full, with vibrant cherry, red and black berry fruits, and earthy and herbal character. It has shown tremendous class on its own and in blends with Cabernet Sauvignon or Merlot, as well as with native varieties such as Mammolo and Canaiolo.

Cabernet Sauvignon

amounts can add more flesh to Sangiovese-based wines.

Merlot

Early-ripening Merlot is exciting in its ability to complement Cabernet and Sangiovese. The wines are soft and full when young, with vibrant ripe berry and plum fruit. Excellent varietals have been made in Chianti Classico, Montalcino, Montepulciano and Bolgheri.

Sangiovese

Cabernet Sauvignon

By the late 1970s Cabernet Sauvignon was single-handedly forging the reputation of Bolgheri. It has since been impressive elsewhere. Varietal examples can be austere initially, but are distinctively herb-scented with a penetrating sweet blackcurrant fruit depth, becoming richer and fuller with age. Small

Vernaccia

Vernaccia

Important only in San Gimignano, the grape shows more character than

most Tuscan whites. Floral and herbal scented, it can become delicately nutty, but only with short oak aging does it show real class.

Chardonnay

The most versatile and popular of the quality international varieties led the white wine-making revolution in Tuscany in the 1980s. The big, broad alcoholic versions include ripe peach, melon and oaky flavours but can be luscious and creamy, if relatively short-lived; others are leaner and more citrussy but sometimes better balanced.

Chardonnay

Other Varieties

The red Canaiolo used to be valued in the governo method and for its ability to soften Sangiovese, but it is now in decline. Malvasia Nera brings colour and a distinctive scent to Sangiovese-based wines, while the white Malvasia is used in the best Vin Santo. Trebbiano Toscano, the most-planted white variety, makes dull wines. Other whites include Sauvignon Blanc, Vermentino, Pinot Blanc and Viognier.

Understanding Tuscan Red and White Wine

You can learn something about a wine simply by looking at the bottle. A derivative of the traditional Bordeaux shape has now replaced the more humble straw-covered flask.

The special seal indicates that this wine has been granted DOCG status.

This estate is a member of the Consorzio del Marchio Storico Chianti Classico.

The name of this small, high-quality estate in the heart of Chianti Classico is given the most emphasis on the label.

In 1995 Chianti Classico finally became a separate DOCG from the rest of Chianti.

Vendemmia means harvest or vintage.

The basic Bordeaux bottle projects a more upmarket image than the cheap and cheerful straw-covered fiaschi. Standard shapes and sizes are also easier to ship and store.

EU regulations now require capsules to be made of tin foil or plastic instead of lead; some are unadorned, others are embossed with the estate name or crest.

. The level of fill usually comes to just below the bottom of the cork, but the gap – or ullage – will slowly increase with age, though it should still remain small.

A single word – the name of this super-Tuscan – dominates the label, reflecting its high profile.

Despite the quality, the wine can only be classified as a humble vino da tavola – though under the new wine laws this will change.

Brown glass is commonly used in Italy as well as the usual olive green.

This bottle is slightly taller due to the use of thicker glass and a deeper punt, also useful for reinforcing a quality image.

WINE CLASSIFICATIONS

There have been a number of changes to Italian wine law in the 1990s as the legislators attempted to incorporate the super-Tuscans. The categories now resemble the French system more closely, with the DOC/DOCG the approximate equivalent of AC:

Vino da Tavola The most basic category without vintage, grape variety or even place of origin specified. The super-Tuscans gave it a special significance, but many will be incorporated into new IGT/DOC categories or existing DOC/DOCGs with revised criteria.

Indicazione Geografiche Tipici (IGT)

A new category, equivalent to the French Vin de Pays, applying to wines which are typical of their region. As well as absorbing some of the premium wines formerly sold as vino da tavola, the IGTs will include a lot of both good and average wines which fall outside the more restrictive DOCs. Labels are expected to bear the description Vino da Indicazione.

Denominazione di Origine Controllata (DOC) The largest category, placing restrictions on geography, grape varieties, yield and aging requirements.

Denominazione di Origine Controllata e Garantita (DOCG)

The top level of Italian classification, with tighter controls on grape varieties, yields and a tasting assessment. Despite its recent revision, it will still fail to include many of Italy's top wines, while endorsing some very ordinary ones. It has been awarded to only 15 wines nationally, of which 6 are from Tuscany. They are: Brunello di Montalcino; Carmignano; Chianti and its 6 sub-zones; Chianti Classico; Vino Nobile di Montepulciano; and Vernaccia di San Gimignano.

THE SUPER-TUSCANS

The wine revolution that began in the 1970s in Italy has resulted in huge advances in the quality of Tuscan wine. The progress in viticulture and wine-making that was being made at this time in Bordeaux, Australia and California could not be embraced in Italy because its legislation was too restrictive.

A small group of quality-minded producers, led by Piero Antinori, decided to bypass tradition by making creative, modern wines that made use of international grape varieties. The first of these, Tignanello and Sassicaia, met with resounding success, and the 1980s saw an explosion of new wines outside the DOC laws that gave a whole new meaning to the term 'vino da tavola' – the only category that could embrace their efforts. Today these so-called 'super-Tuscans' fetch some of the highest prices of all Italian wines.

What's in a Name?

The surge of consumer interest in these modestly designated premium wines led producers to create still more new labels in order to get a better return on their investment. The resulting plethora of fancy names (nomi da fantasia) needed some classification: the designation of Predicato (now called Capitolare) was not a resounding success.

Now the authorities have been forced to accommodate the super-Tuscans: new laws are beginning to take effect which could mean eventually that the wines are seen less as a distinct group but more in the context of specific new or existing DOCs.

However, the main criterion for the consumer should still be the name of the producer. The following is a list of some of the best producers of reds, followed by the name of the wine:

Predominantly Sangiovese
Boscarelli – Boscarelli
Felsina Berardenga – Fontalloro
Fontodi – Flaccianello
Isole e Olena – Cepparello
Montevertine – Le Pergole Torte
Poggio Scalette – Il Carbonaione
Sangiovese and Cabernet blends
Antinori – Tignanello
Fonterutoli – Concerto
Querciabella – Camartina
Valtellina – Convivio
Predominantly Cabernet
Antinori – Solaia
Castello dei Rampolla – Sammarco
Tenuta dell'Ornellaia – Ornellaia
Tenuta San Guido – Sassicaia
Merlot
Avignonesi – Grifi
Tenuta dell'Ornellaia – Masseto
Castello di Ama – L'Apparita

How to Choose Tuscan Wine

On the label below – from Brunello di Montalcino Vigna di Pianrosso, Ciacci Piccolomini d'Aragona – the DOCG is given precedence over the producer's name. This should hint at the wine style, but it is down to the producer and vintage to distinguish one bottle from another. A good producer, by implication, shouldn't make bad wines whatever the vintage, so ultimately it is the estate or grower that really matters – the location of the vineyards, planting density, yields, vineyard management and wine-making skills all play a part in determining the quality of the wine.

The family coat of arms represents lineage often traceable to the Renaissance, though commercial production of Brunello may date from only a decade or so ago.

Vigna di Pianrosso is a favoured vineyard site in Castelnuovo dell'Abate in the south-east corner of the Brunello zone.

The DOCG.

BRUNELLO DI MONTALCINO
DENOMINAZIONE DI ORIGINE CONTROLLATA E GARANTITA
– Vigna di Pianrosso –
1990
RED WINE. ESTATE BOTTLED BY
CIACCI PICCOLOMINI D'ARAGONA
di GIUSEPPE BIANCHINI MONTALCINO ITALIA
PRODUCT OF ITALY
NET CONT. 750 ML   ALC. 14% BY VOL.

The vintage. 1990 was a marvellous year in Tuscany. This wine is ready to drink but will still continue to improve.

The producer's name.

14% alcohol by volume is not uncommon for this powerful red wine.

GLOSSARY

Alberese Limestone-rich schist-like soil.

Azienda Agricola Wine estate where the wine is both produced and bottled at source.

Barrique Bordeaux barrel of 225 litres, usually made from French or American oak; in Italy it can also refer to any small barrel, from wood of diverse origin.

Commune The smallest political sub-division, named after the major town or village in the area.

Enologist Wine scientist. In Tuscany, high-profile consultants have had a radical influence on wine-making – most of the quality estates have been given and continue to receive some advice. Some of the most respected include: Niccolò d'Afflitto, Franco Bernabei, Maurizio Castelli, Carlo Ferrini, Vittorio Fiore, Giulio Gambelli, Attilio Pagli, Luigi Peira and Giacomo Tachis.

Fattoria Farm, a title used by some wine estates; usually larger than a PODERE.

Frazione Outlying ward within a COMMUNE; a distinct character in its wines can sometimes be discerned.

Galestro Highly prized soil of friable clay with a high calcareous content; also a commercial neutral white wine.

Governo Traditional Chianti technique of adding dried grapes to already fermented wine. Increases the alcohol, helps start the malolactic fermentation but can add a little spritz to young wines. Still given credibility by one or two top consultants.

Mesoclimate/Microclimate Correctly used, mesoclimate refers to the climate of a distinct geographical area, microclimate to conditions surrounding the vine itself.

Normale Non-RISERVA wine.

Organic Viticulture Avoidance of chemical fertilizers, herbicides and pesticides and certain additives in the vineyard and wine-making.

Passito Often sweet wine made from dried grapes.

Podere Farm or small estate. Many produce olive oil, jam and honey as well as wine.

Riserva Term for a superior wine, usually given with more aging and greater percentage of alcohol.

Terroir Natural physical environment in which the grapes are grown – its expression in the wine depends on the quality of the fruit, the naturalness of the wine-making process and how typical of the zone an individual site is.

Varietal Wine from a single grape variety in a wine; or its characteristics.

Understanding Vin Santo

Tuscany's 'holy wine' is more famous, rich and luscious than that of Umbria or Trentino. Traditionally a peasants' drink for special occasions, some modern examples are still made in this relatively light, semi-sweet style, with oxidized flavours. But a (very expensive) handful of others are rich, concentrated and full of dried apricots, candied fruits, citrus peel or marmalade, with some intense nutty character too.

The clear bottle is used to show off the colour of the wine even though it provides less protection against damaging light and heat than a dark brown or olive green bottle.

A gold-coloured capsule reinforces the image of a sweet wine

Although a vintage is shown here, Vin Santo can be the product of more than one harvest.

The 50cl bottle is gaining in popularity and is just the right amount for two.

One of the handful of truly outstanding Vin Santo producers.

How Vin Santo is Made

The production of Vin Santo ensures the continuation of a wine style important in the ancient world – that from dried or raisined grapes. Malvasia and Trebbiano grapes are dried on trays or hung from the rafters, for at least three months. There must be good ventilation to ensure that the grapes dry without succumbing to malevolent rot.

After the grapes have fully shrivelled, they are fermented for two or three months in small oak barrels (*carattelli*). The process is very slow and imprecise, and may even restart with seasonal temperature changes. The wine is then aged for four to six years but remains in contact with a *madre* or mother – a little wine that is enriched from year to year – and is concentrated in yeasts. *Passito* wines are high in alcohol (15–16 per cent), and once bottled can continue to improve for a long time.

VINTAGES

Despite the huge strides made by some quality producers, there is still much wine that will not last, let alone improve, for longer than three or four years.

However, the very best Chianti Riserva, super-Tuscan, Brunello or Vino Nobile, should last for ten years. Fine Chianti (especially Classico and Rufina) and Rosso di Montalcino and Montepulciano can provide superb drinking and much better value for money with less than half that age.

1996 High in promise. Looks set to continue the run of good to excellent vintages to a fourth year.

1995 A cool summer was saved by a warm sunny October. Generally a very good year, although quantities are down.

1994 As in 93, rain did its worst but the grapes were already in good shape. Those least affected again managed real quality.

1993 A damp harvest but despite the early pessimism, careful selection has resulted in reds with excellent colour, fruit and structure.

1992 A miserable vintage. Little premium wine was made, so the Chianti Normale and Rosso di Montalcino benefited – these are charming wines, perfumed if sometimes initially austere.

1991 Somewhat variable and initially poorly received in the shadow of 1990. Some intense reds for medium-term keeping.

1990 An outstanding vintage throughout Tuscany. Drink Chianti Normale now and start on the Riservas. Some better super-Tuscans and Brunello/Vino Nobile still need more time.

1989 A lighter than average vintage. Some wines still display a certain charm, but too many lacked real concentration and should have been drunk by now.

1988 Shares something of both the firmness and quality of Bordeaux and Burgundy in 1988. Only exceptional Chianti Normale is still good, while Riserva, super-Tuscans and Brunello/Vino Nobile should all be drunk now or soon.

1987 A difficult vintage – there is little else worth drinking.

1986 Chianti Riserva has aged beautifully as have a number of super-Tuscans. Drink now.

1985 Highly rated from the outset but not all these firmly structured wines have sufficient rich, ripe fruit.

Older Vintages 1983 and 82 were good vintages but most wines are now tired, a handful of Brunello and super-Tuscans excepted. Older fine bottles are generally very scarce, but might come from 1975 (Brunello), 71 or 70.

Hams and salume *are always hung up for storage and for display throughout Tuscany.*

MATCHING WINE AND FOOD

Tuscan wines come into their own with food. The simple char-grilled meats and the rich stews of the region make the perfect foil for serious red wines.

Look for producers listed in the back of this guide when choosing what to drink, and experiment with different styles of wine to go with what you are eating.

You might like to try the light, inoffensive Galestro and the fragrant Moscadello di Montalcino as pleasant *aperitivi;* fragrant, chilled dry rosés from Bolgheri and Carmignano for outdoor lunches; characterful Vernaccia di San Gimignano and more full-bodied Chardonnay and Sauvignon super-Tuscan whites with char-grilled fish and chicken; lighter Chianti, Rosso di Montalcino, and Rosso di Montepulciano with mixed *antipasti,* simple bread soups and grilled meats; serious Chianti Classico Riserva, Brunello di Montalcino, Vino Nobile di Montepulciano, and Cabernet- and Sangiovese-based super-Tuscans with *bistecca alla fiorentina, pappardelle alla lepre,* wild boar, winter stews and aged *pecorino* cheese.

Vin Santo with hard, crunchy *cantuccini* biscuits is still the classic finish to a Tuscan meal, while the new wave dessert wines, in some cases made with late-harvested grapes affected by *muffa nobile* (noble rot or *Botrytis cinerea*) are well worth trying.

Regional Food

The cuisine of Tuscany is essentially an unadorned country diet, based on fresh seasonal ingredients, bread and extra-virgin olive oil.

No meal, no snack even, is complete without bread. Made from a dense unsalted sourdough, preferably baked in a wood-fired oven, it emerges gloriously fragrant, with a hard crust and a chewy, resistant interior that goes perfectly with Tuscan cured meats. Toasted over a wood fire, rubbed with a cut clove of garlic, and dribbled with extra-virgin Tuscan olive oil, it becomes the simplest, most delicious of appetizers, *fettunta,* while stale Tuscan bread is the basis for an outstanding range of *zuppe di pane* (bread soups) made with fresh seasonal vegetables.

Olive oil, the backbone of the Mediterranean diet, is at its most delicious when made from olives grown in the high wine hills of Tuscany. Here the olive tree is at the limit of its viability but, as with vines, the struggle to survive can produce superlative results. Single-estate extra-virgin oils from Chianti Classico, Carmignano and Rufina are nothing short of pure liquid green-gold (and fetch prices to match); these are the Grands Crus of the oil world, as different from ordinary supermarket olive oil as the super-Tuscan wines are from everyday straw-covered flasks of Chianti.

Seasonal Food

Freshness is all in the Tuscan diet and it is impossible not to eat seasonally. This means, for example, that early spring brings *fave* (broad beans), best enjoyed raw with nuggets of young *pecorino* cheese; early summer is the season of tender *asparagi* (green asparagus) and other fine vegetable and fruit; by late summer knowledgeable mushroom hunters can gather a feast of *funghi* in the woods; and winter is the season for *cavolo nero,* a characteristic, slightly bitter winter green that is indispensable for the classic *ribollita* (see box opposite).

In order to see, to feel, to smell what is fresh and in season, don't miss visiting local weekly markets. Go just for the pleasure of looking or to pick out the seasonal best if you are self-catering or buying for a picnic.

Eating Out

Wherever you find yourself in Tuscany there is never any shortage of good restaurants to choose from. They range from simple, local *osterie* and *trattorie* serving inexpensive *cucina casalinga* (home cooking) to refined and sophisticated establishments that rank among the most exclusive (and expensive) in the country.

Traditional Tuscan favourites are available (with local variations) throughout the region, while more refined restaurants often present *cucina toscana rivisitata* – modifications of traditional dishes in lighter and more creative guises. You may not always be shown a menu; instead, the waiter may simply reel off a list of dishes to pick from.

In city and country kitchens alike, an open fire is one of the principal means of cooking. Even in summer great open fires blaze away and all manner of meats are cooked over them or on revolving spits, the classic Tuscan *girarrosto*. Don't miss the famous *bistecca alla fiorentina*, a massive T-bone steak from the Chianina breed of cattle, or, less famous but no less delicious, pork or veal chops, meaty pork *salsicce* (sausages) or pick-up with-your-fingers food such as *rosticciana* (pork ribs).

Most restaurants in Tuscany should, in theory, offer an acceptable *vino della casa* (house wine); they will also have a *lista dei vini* (wine list) with more interesting, superior bottlings from the finest local wine zones. This may not even be offered to you unless you ask to see it.

Shops like this general store in Castellina in Chianti will sell only seasonal fresh fruit and vegetables, many of which are locally produced.

REGIONAL SPECIALITIES

ANTIPASTI
Antipasti toscani Usually means a selection of cured Tuscan meats (*salame toscano, finocchiona, prosciutto*) accompanied by *crostini* and *fettunta* (see below).
Bacelli con pecorino Broad beans (*fave*) served raw when young and small with nuggets of fresh *pecorino* cheese.
Crostini Rounds of toasted bread, typically spread with a mixture of chicken livers, capers and anchovies, or with chopped vegetables dressed with olive oil.
Fettunta or *bruschetta* Slice of Tuscan unsalted bread, toasted over a fire, rubbed with garlic and dribbled with extra-virgin olive oil. May have a topping such as chopped fresh tomato.
Finocchiona Tuscany's finest salami, loosely textured and rather soft and crumbly, flavoured with wild fennel seeds.
Panzanella A refreshing summer 'bread salad', made from stale Tuscan bread soaked in water, squeezed dry and then mixed with tomatoes, onion, cucumber, basil and other herbs, and seasoned with a light dressing of vinegar and olive oil.
Pinzimonio Platter of raw seasonal vegetables, such as tomatoes, red peppers, fennel, celery, carrots, to be dipped into olive oil, salt and pepper.
Prosciutto toscano Salty, strongly flavoured air-cured ham, seasoned with garlic and a good dose of black pepper.

Salame toscano Large, softly textured pure pork salami made from highly seasoned lean meat with large cubes of fat set in the mixture.
Salame di cinghiale Chewy, tasty salami made from wild boar.

PRIMI PIATTI
Pappa al pomodoro Fresh tomato and Tuscan bread soup: a regional summer classic.
Pappardelle alle lepre or *al cinghiale* Thick, hand-cut ribbon noodles, typically served with a rich, dark sauce made from hare stewed in wine, or with a *ragù* (meat sauce) made from wild boar.
Pici or *pinci* Thickish, handmade spaghetti-type pasta, made with flour, water and salt only, traditionally seasoned with a sauce of breadcrumbs, garlic, olive oil and hot chillis; today more often served either *al aglione* (with a tomato, garlic and bay sauce) or *al ragù di anatra* (duck sauce). Speciality of Montalcino and Montepulciano, and thus a fitting partner to lighter Rosso wines from those zones.
Ribollita Hearty, 're-boiled' winter minestrone made with beans, vegetables and Tuscan bread.

SECONDI PIATTI
Arista di maiale Roast loin of pork, flavoured with herbs and garlic.
Bistecca alla fiorentina Classic Tuscan T-bone steak, from the Chianina breed of cattle, char-grilled and seasoned only with salt, pepper and olive oil. This expensive (you usually pay by weight) speciality demands one of the fine red super-Tuscan wines, or a bottle of mature

Brunello di Montalcino or Chianti Classico Riserva.
Cinghiale in umido Stew of wild boar, rich, meaty and gamy.
Costoletta di maiale or *di vitello* Char-grilled pork or veal chop, cooked over a wood fire, sprinkled with salt, herbs and garlic, and served with a wedge of lemon.
Faraona Guinea fowl, usually roasted.
Salsicce Meaty, tasty sausages, grilled or pan-fried with white wine.
Scottiglia Mixture of meats, including chicken, rabbit, pork, veal or lamb, stewed in olive oil, garlic and herbs, often served on a slice of bread.
Stracotto al Chianti Whole piece of beef or veal, slow-cooked in Chianti wine. Best accompanied with mature Chianti Classico Riserva.

CONTORNI
Fagioli White beans, a Tuscan favourite, often served *all'uccelletto* (stewed with tomato and sage), and more simply with oil as an accompaniment to *Bistecca alla fiorentina*.

FORMAGGI
Pecorino Ewe's milk cheese, either *dolce* (fresh) or *stagionato* (aged).

DOLCI
Cantuccini Hard, twice-baked almond biscuits, traditionally from the Carmignano region; *de rigueur* to dip into a glass of sweet Vin Santo.
Crostata Fresh fruit and jam tart.

The wine regions in Tuscany are among the most attractive and welcoming areas to visit – for the serious wine lover as well as for the amateur.

SUMMARY OF TOURS

Carmignano Unspoiled rural wine zone, featuring Medici villas, Etruscan tombs and an optional detour to Vinci, the birthplace of the artist Leonardo da Vinci.

Chianti Rufina and Pomino At the foothills of the Apennines, a tour of one of Chianti's most distinguished sub-zones, together with a visit to the tiny historic wine region of Pomino.

Chianti Classico The 'Black Rooster' wine country, divided into three separate tours, covering the historic area between Florence and Siena.

San Gimignano An exploration of the gently rolling hill country surrounding the City of Beautiful Towers.

Bolgheri and the Etruscan Coast Tiny and little-visited new wine zone, including the regions of Montescudaio and Suvereto.

Montalcino The home of Tuscany's most prestigious, blockbuster wine, surrounding a fascinating medieval town.

Montepulciano A tour beginning in Tuscany's finest Renaissance wine town, and exploring its varied countryside.

Touring Tuscany

Wine is part and parcel of the Tuscan way of life, as essential as bread and extra-virgin olive oil. Its greatest wine regions lie within easy reach of Florence and Siena. Chianti Classico and Chianti Rufina, Carmignano, San Gimignano, Montalcino and Montepulciano can be visited comfortably from these two great centres of art and culture. Only tiny Bolgheri, on the Tuscan coast, stands apart, an emerging wine zone already producing world-class wines.

The concept of wine tourism is a relatively new one, but producers are making great strides in opening their estates – as well as their wines – to the visitor. Numerous attractive wine towns have been designated *città del vino*, or city of wine, an initiative that serves to co-ordinate wine-related events (tel 0577/271556; fax 0577/271595 for more information). The most common of the various different tourist organizations is APT (Azienda di Promozione Turistica), which offers general advice and free maps and accommodation lists. In the smaller villages the Pro Loco performs much the same function, while during the summer months even smaller informal booths open up. The national Movimento del Turismo del Vino is particularly well organized in Tuscany, publishing a booklet giving details of scores of important estates (tel 0574/582426 or 0577/848277; fax 0574/582428 or 0577/849356).

Spring and autumn are the best seasons to visit the wine country, the former because the countryside is fresh and just bursting into life, the latter as it is the time of the grape harvest. Wine producers themselves may not be at home in August (when just about all of Italy heads for either sea or mountains), while winters can be bitterly cold.

In all the areas covered, there are good hotels, from budget to super-luxurious, as well as scores of fine places for *agriturismo*, the broad term for farmhouse holidays, which involves staying on a working farm or estate in rooms, an apartment or villa. There are no hotel listings for Florence and Siena, as both have so many good or reasonable options – it is best to choose one to suit your needs.

This book also points you to the best restaurants, ranging from local *osterie* to elegant world-class establishments. Remember that all restaurants close at least one day a week, so it is best to telephone in advance. The cheapest way to sample the wines of the region, however, is by the glass at an *enoteca* (wine shop) or a wine bar.

Most of the wine tours involve driving on a mixture of surfaced roads and unpaved tracks. Italy has severe laws relating to drinking and driving, so if you plan to visit estates and taste wines, plan accordingly.

Florence

Florence, the city of art, is rightly one of Italy's great destinations, and most who visit Tuscany will wish to spend some days here, exploring its museums, galleries and churches. However, wine tourists do not live by art alone, and this prosperous Renaissance city and modern metropolis has no shortage of stylish restaurants and local *osterie*, serving innovative cuisine and Tuscan country food alike. Elegant city wine bars as well as atmospheric *fiaschetterie, buche* and *vinerie* – the traditional bars of the old city – provide plenty of wine-tasting opportunities. And as Florence is the capital of both province and region, the finest wines from Tuscany's outlying wine zones all find their way here, so there are plenty of good places to buy wine.

Some of Florence's countless wine bars are little more than 'holes in the-wall' but all provide a wonderful opportunity to rub shoulders with the locals while sampling the wines of the region.

Florence Fact File

Here are just some of the many restaurants in the city. Most of the bars listed serve inexpensive meals.

Information
APT
Via Manzoni 16. Tel 055/23320; fax 055/2346284.

Ufficio Informazioni Turistiche
Via Cavour 1r. Tel 055/290832.

Associazione Agriturist Toscana
Piazza S. Firenze 3. Tel 055/287838; fax: 055/2302285
Agency providing information and publications on farmhouse holidays in Tuscany.

Markets
Mercato Centrale
Via dell'Ariento – Mon–Sat
Mercato di Sant'Ambrogio
Piazza Ghiberti – Mon–Sat

Festivals and Events
Florence boasts an important gastronomic festival, *Firenze a tavola con l'Europa,* in the second half of March – a trade fair and a public showcase.

Enoteche and Bars
Antico Noé
Volta di S. Piero 6r.
Located under the vaulted arches of San Piero for nearly 200 years, this is a Florentine institution, serving a fair selection of wines.

Cantinetta Antinori
Piazza degli Antinori 3.
Try such classics as Antinori's Tignanello, Solaia, Guado al Tasso and Muffa della Sala in this stylish city centre wine bar.

Casa del Vino
Via dell'Ariento 16r.
Locals' bar between San Lorenzo and the Mercato Centrale, with quality wines in crystal glasses.

Il Cantinone del Gallo Nero
Via S. Spirito 6r.
Located in the cellars of a 16th-century palace, with a good selection of Chiantis.

Fiaschetteria Nuvoli
Piazza dell'Olio 15.
Tiny *buca* near the Duomo, serving local wines. Try the Riservas from Grevepesa.

Enoteca Pitti Gola e Cantina
Piazza Pitti 16.
Good, stylish wine shop, with occasional tutored wine-tastings in conjunction with Arcigola, the Slow Food Association.

Cantinetta da Verrazzano
Via dei Tavolini 18r.
Centrally located; wines from the Verrazzano estate and bread from the wood-fired oven.

Le Volpi e l'Uva
Piazza de'Rossi.
Little-known wines from the whole of Italy by the glass and for sale by the bottle or case.

Where to Eat
Cibreo
Via dei Macci 118r. Tel 055/2341100; fax 055/244966. ⓁⓁ
Classic Florentine restaurant offering well-prepared traditional food. In adjacent Piazza Ghiberti, the Osteria Cibreo serves tasty meals at budget prices.

Ristorante Dino
Via Ghibellina 51r. Tel 055/241452; fax 055/241378. ⓁⓁ
Family-run favourite located in a 14th-century palace serving traditional food. The proprietor is hugely knowledgeable about Tuscan wines, so ask his advice.

Ristorante Oliviero
Via delle Terme 51r. Tel 055/287643. ⓁⓁ
A stylish and popular restaurant in the city centre.

Enoteca Pinchiorri
Via Ghibellina 87. Tel 055/242777; fax 055/244983. ⓁⓁⓁ
Cucina creativa, mixing Tuscan influences with French *nouvelle.* Prices are astronomical, although the set menus are good value. Probably the best wine list in Italy.

The cultivation at the Carmignano zone's leading estate, Capezzana, is typical of the zone. Vineyards are interspersed with olive groves and cypress trees on the northern flanks of the Montalbano hills, west of Florence. In fact, the high-quality olive oil of Carmignano is almost as prized as its wines, and Capezzana's fruity and elegant example, produced on the estate's own *frantoio* (traditional stone-ground olive oil mill), is one of Tuscany's best. The vineyards running south from the estate buildings are relatively young; the narrow space between the rows of vines and the high density of plants per hectare is typical of much of the new planting in Tuscany. The Villa di Capezzana is visible to the right, while spread out along the ridge are parts of the winery and *frantoio*; the building with the lattice windows is the the *vinsantaia*, where grapes are laid out on cane mats, known locally as *gratucci* or *stuoie*, to dry slowly during the autumn months for the production of traditional Vin Santo.

The vineyards of the Capezzana estate take full advantage of the hilly nature of the region.

Carmignano

The tiny wine zone of Carmignano lies on the northern flank of the Montalbano hills 20km (12 miles) west of Florence, spread over an area that once comprised a walled Medici hunting preserve called the Barco Reale. Although so close to Florence and the industrial centres of Prato and Pistoia, it remains an area of great natural beauty and history, rich in Etruscan remains, and dominated by splendid Medici villas. There are few producers, but more of them are now making a range of wines that includes light but sappy Barco Reale reds and fruity Vin Ruspo rosés, styles that were invented by Capezzana, the zone's leading estate. Most important, however, are the stylish, ageworthy Sangiovese-based reds that seamlessly integrate a measure of Cabernet Sauvignon.

The Tour

Head west out of Florence, following signs to Pistoia (S66). About 8km (5 miles) out of the city, turn left to Signa and, once there, follow the signs right (just before the railway underpass) to Artimino on a quiet road that follows the Arno for a stretch, then winds up steeply through woods.

Artimino lies on the edge of the Carmignano wine country, a wholly intact, tiny medieval hamlet, the surrounding vineyards and olive groves extending over the flank of hills looking down to Florence. Separated from the village by a long avenue, a fine Medici villa, known as the 'Villa of a Hundred Chimneys', today houses an archaeological museum and a luxury hotel. The modern winemaking facility of the Artimino estate is situated below the town. With over 80ha of vineyards, it is the zone's largest producer, source of fruity Barco Reale and deeper Carmignano Riserva Medicea.

From Artimino, head in the direction of Poggio a Caiano, pausing at the village of Comeana to look at its impressive Etruscan tombs dating from the 7th century BC, which can be found on the Calavria estate. The vineyards and winery to the left just outside Comeana belong to the Ambra estate, a small family operation producing wines of real quality and class – the Carmignano Riserva Le Vigne Alte can be stunning.

Poggio a Caiano itself is a rather dull town on the main road that trundles on to Pistoia, noted mainly for its rather grandiose Medici villa set in lovely gardens. From Poggio, return into the wine hills to Carmignano, a small but strategic town much fought over in the Middle Ages in the frequent struggles between Florence, Pistoia and Prato. Although the town gives its name to the wine zone, there

TOUR SUMMARY

An excursion from Florence into unspoiled and still little-visited wine country, with visits to Medici villas at Artimino, Poggio a Caiano and Capezzana, and Etruscan tombs at Comeana. Includes an optional detour to Vinci, the birthplace of the artist Leonardo da Vinci.

Distance covered 55km (35 miles).

Time needed 3 hours for the main tour; allow 1 hour extra for Vinci.

Terrain The tour follows good surfaced roads, although the hill country between Capezzana and Bacchereto is steep.

Hotels Although within easy reach of Florence, there are choices in the region to suit all pockets. There is also good *agriturismo* in Bacchereto, Artimino and Serravalle.

Restaurants Artimino has one of the finest country restaurants in Tuscany. Elsewhere in the wine zone there are good local *trattorie*.

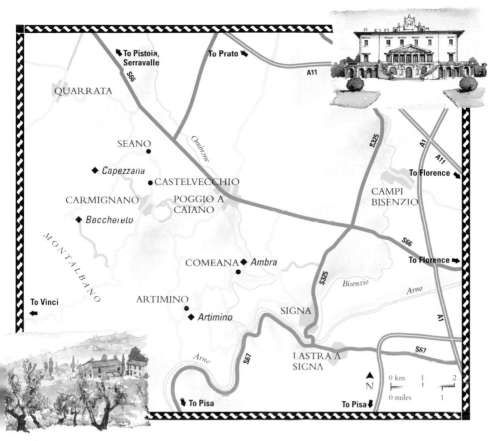

To Pistoia, Serravalle

To Prato

A11

QUARRATA

SEANO

Ombrone

◆ Capezzana

●CASTELVECCHIO

CARMIGNANO

POGGIO A CAIANO

◆ Bacchereto

MONTALBANO

COMEANA ◆ Ambra

To Vinci

ARTIMINO

◆ Artimino

SIGNA

S325

To Florence

CAMPI BISENZIO

S66

To Florence

Bisenzio

Arno

Arno

S67

LASTRA A SIGNA

N

0 km 1 2

0 miles 1

To Pisa

To Pisa

are few wine-tasting opportunities here, except during the *Fiera di San Michele* in September. For local wines and exceptional pastries, cakes and *biscotti*, try the famous Pasticceria Bellini on Via Roma.

Capezzana, the dominant producer of the zone, lies above Carmignano off the road from Seano. Documentary evidence shows that wine and olive oil have been produced on the estate since at least AD 804, although the ancient Etruscans and Romans almost certainly cultivated both here centuries earlier. Today, the Contini Bonacossi's fine estate Villa di Capezzana Riserva, Villa di Trefiano and the Bordeaux-blend super-Tuscan Ghiaie della Furba are among Carmignano's best wines.

Continue through the high hills round to the Bacchereto estate. The Medici built a hunting lodge here, on the fringe of the Barco Reale, and today this villa is the source of good Carmignano and Vin Santo, as well as olive oil and honey.

The wine tour ends in Bacchereto, but an alternative excursion can be made over the pretty wooded slopes of the Montalbano range to Vinci, birthplace of Leonardo. The museum there contains fascinating models of inventions and machines recreated from the great Renaissance humanist's drawings.

Map illustrations: (above) the Medici villa at Poggio a Caiano; (below) an olive grove in Carmignano.

Carmignano Fact File

Close enough to explore from Florence, the wine country makes a pleasant break from city sightseeing.

Information

APT
Via Luigi Muzzi 51, 50047
Prato. Tel 0574/35141.

Congregazione dei Vini di Carmignano
c/o Comune di Carmignano,
50042 Carmignano PO. Tel
055/8712002; fax 055/8712008.

Markets

Carmignano – Tuesday
Poggio a Caiano – Thursday

Festivals and Events

Carmignano's *Fiera di San Michele* takes place at the end of September. Quarrata hosts a wine festival during the first week of September.

Enoteche and Bars

Until the *enoteca* in Carmignano town reopens, there is no shop in the zone with a comprehensive selection of wines.
Enoteca Le Cantine del Redi
50040 Artimino PO.
A congenial place to sample the wines of the zone. Evenings only.

Bar Alimentari Peruzzi
Via Martiri 21, 50040 Artimino
PO.

Where to Stay and Eat

**Albergo La Bussola –
Ristorante da Gino Ⓗ Ⓡ**
Via V. Fiorentina 328 (S966),
51030 Quarrata PO. Tel & fax
0573/743128. Ⓛ
Traditional *osteria* en route to
Pistoia: outstanding pasta,
mushrooms and game, with a
selection of the best wines of
Carmignano. There are also 10
rooms with bathrooms.

Da Delfina Ⓡ
Via della Chiesa 1, 50040
Artimino PO. Tel 055/8718074;
fax 055/8718175. Ⓛ Ⓛ
One of Tuscany's outstanding
country restaurants. Elegantly
prepared dishes of seasonal
ingredients, wild herbs and
superbly cooked meats.

**Hotel Paggeria Medicea –
Ristorante Biagio Pignatta
Ⓗ Ⓡ**
Viale Papa Giovanni XXIII,
50040 Artimino PO. Tel 055/
8718081 (restaurant 055/
8718086); fax 055/8718080.
Ⓛ Ⓛ Ⓛ
Elegant country hotel with
swimming pool and a good
restaurant. *Agriturismo* apartments
available by the week.

Antica Trattoria Sanesi Ⓡ

Via Arione 33, 50055 Lastra a
Signa FI. Tel & fax 055/
8720234. Ⓛ Ⓛ
Historic *trattoria* serving good
pasta, meticulously prepared
bistecca, and other grilled meats
(try the *rosticciana*). House wine
is fine, but there is also a small
selection of Chianti Riserva.

La Cantina di Toia Ⓡ
Via Toia 12, 50040 Bacchereto
PO. Tel & fax 055/8717135.
Ⓛ Ⓛ
Located in the 13th-century
house of Lucia di Zoso,
grandmother of Leonardo da
Vinci, this *trattoria* offers
sophisticated creative cuisine.

Agriturismo

Fattoria di Bacchereto
Via Fontemorana 179, 50040
Bacchereto PO. Tel & fax 055/
8717191.
Farmhouse accommodation and
meals in the high wine hills.

Fattoria Le Poggiolo
Via di Treggiaia 13, Loc. Ponte,
51030 Serravalle PT. Tel & fax
0573/51071.
At the far end of the Montalbano
range, this friendly wine estate
offers rooms or an apartment for
rent. Meals from farm produce,
enjoyed with the Barsi family.

Wines and Wine Villages

The towns and villages in Carmignano are of little interest in themselves, save for their Medici villas. The countryside is the real draw, ideal for quiet, relaxed exploring.

Artimino Tiny medieval hamlet, with a fine Medici villa incorporating a museum of local Roman and Etruscan finds. Also home to a wine estate of the same name.

Carmignano DOC/DOCG
Wine zone taking its name from the uninspiring town at its centre. The vineyards are planted on the hills or sloping plains at low altitudes (50–200m/165–650ft). Production is small and wines are usually lower in acidity but

with firmer tannin than in Chianti Classico. The DOCG applies only to the Sangiovese-based red topped up with Cabernet Sauvignon – though austere when young, the Riservas in particular are ageworthy and refined. The DOC now applies to: Barco Reale, a delightful early-drinking red; Vin Ruspo rosé; and Vin Santo.
Best producers: AMBRA, ARTIMINO, BACCHERETO, CAPEZZANA, *Le Farnete, Iolanda Pratesi.*

Chianti Montalbano DOCG
One of the 7 Chianti zones, centred on the higher and cooler Montalbano range spreading north and west of Carmignano. The wines are generally light with highish acidity.

Comeana Small village close to the quality estate of Ambra. The Calavria wine estate is the site of Etruscan tombs; excavations are being carried out to a much larger burial mound.

Poggio a Caiano Market town, home to the famous Medici villa built for Lorenzo Il Magnifico in the 15th century.

Chianti Rufina
and Pomino

Rising above the Arno and Sieve valleys, a steep bank of hills north-east of Florence comprises the wine zones of Chianti Rufina, the smallest of the seven Chianti zones, and Pomino, a tiny but historic wine enclave. Once a summer retreat for Florentine nobles, it is an area of great beauty and history, whose relatively cool climate results in wines that are austere and structured, with great potential for aging. A pleasant base in itself, the region also makes an enjoyable excursion from Florence, and can be combined with a visit to the fortified Abbey of Vallombrosa.

The Sieve, seen here from the Fornacce vineyard of Selvapiana, is one of the two rivers that dominate the Chianti Rufina zone – the other is the Arno.

The Tour

Pontassieve, the starting point of the tour, is located where the Sieve river joins the Arno, and has long been a commercially strategic crossroads. It is the centre for large-scale merchants who traditionally have blended and bottled easy-to-drink bulk wines for national and international markets. The town was severely damaged in World War Two and few monuments remain, though the restored Medici bridge, built in 1555, still spans the Sieve further upriver.

Follow the Arno downriver to Sieci. The large modern bottling plant and warehouse just before Sieci belong to Frescobaldi, possibly the largest private family vineyard owner in Italy, with over 850ha of vineyards in the region. Vinification and aging of the finest estate wines take place on its Nipozzano and Tenuta di Pomino estates.

In Sieci, turn right at the town square along the Via dello Stracchino; after the railway line the road begins to rise gently into the Rufina hills. This is not an intensive wine zone: on the lower ground, cereals and sunflowers predominate, and higher up, olives and vines give way to large tracts of woodland. Frescobaldi's Poggio a Remole estate is located along this stretch, though the wine that bears this name is no longer an estate Chianti Rufina, as it now includes grapes from outside the zone.

The road continues to climb through dense woodland, olive groves and lines of cypress trees, and looking back, there are impressive views down to the Arno Valley and the hills of Colli Fiorentini. A few miles further on the right is the Bossi estate, centred on a 15th-century villa remodelled in the 19th century in a rather grandiose French style. Today, under the direction of young, energetic Marchese Bernardo Gondi, previously tannic, rather old-fashioned reds are becoming more approachable; the estate's Vin Santo is superlative.

TOUR SUMMARY

Circular tour beginning in Pontassieve, and exploring these little-known zones through unspoiled hill country; an optional excursion can be made to the Abbey of Vallombrosa.

Distance covered 45km (30 miles) for the main tour.

Time needed 3 hours. Allow 2 hours extra for a visit to Vallombrosa.

Terrain Surfaced roads are all good, although driving, especially in the steep hills, is leisurely.

Hotels While the zones are both easily reached from Florence, there are acceptable hotels in the region, as well as good *agriturismo*.

Restaurants There are several local *trattorie* along the suggested wine route.

Continue into the hills toward the town of Rufina, through country planted mainly with olives. After Monterifrassine, turn right to descend through the vineyards of one of the zone's larger producers, Galiga e Vetrice, whose Villa di Vetrice wines are excellent value and more consistent than in the past. The 13th-century watchtower, one of many in these hills, is evidence of the strategic importance of the area in times past. The final estate here is Basciano, where Renzo Masi has increased quality in recent years. One of the zone's best restaurants, Osteria La Casellina, is located nearby in this flank of hills.

The busy, if hardly attractive, market town of Rufina gives its name to the wine zone. Its most notable monument is the 16th-century Villa Poggio Reale. Said to have been inspired by a design by Michelangelo, this beautiful Renaissance villa already houses a wine museum and is being restored as a promotional centre for the wines of Chianti Rufina and Pomino.

Before continuing to Pomino, head south to Rufina's leading estate, Selvapiana, an imposing yellow Renaissance villa on hills overlooking the left bank of the Sieve. Once the summer residence of the Bishops of Florence, half of the villa was destroyed at the end of World War Two; today it is ably run by Dr Francesco Giuntini, who has done much to make the zone better known. Winemaker Federico

Masseti, with help from the formidable consultant Franco Bernabei, has made Selvapiana one of the most exciting estates in Tuscany. But these are not easy-drinking wines: the basic Rufina is vibrant and intense, the long-lived Riserva adds more depth and structure, while Bucerchiale is outstanding. Fornacce is a new, already highly prized Cru.

Return through Rufina on the road to Forlì; soon after leaving the town, take the road on the right to the village of Pomino. This is one of Italy's smallest DOC zones, but it deserves its separate status, not simply because it was singled out in Cosimo III de Medici's grand-ducal decree of 1716, but because it has, for more than a hundred years, produced wines with their own distinct character, primarily from non-Tuscan grapes such as Pinot Noir, Merlot, Cabernet Sauvignon, Pinot Grigio and Chardonnay.

Frescobaldi used to be the sole producer of Pomino wines. Now, however, Dr Giuntini of Selvapiana leases 6ha of vineyards from the Petrognano estate, located before the village of Pomino, and is producing an attractive Pomino Petrognano from Sangiovese, Cabernet and Merlot.

Pomino itself is little more than a high, isolated mountain hamlet, almost entirely surrounded by its vineyards. Don't miss the beautiful 13th-century Romanesque Pieve di San Bartolomeo, or the Macelleria Perigli for fine *salumi* for a picnic overlooking the vineyards.

Selvapiana's vendita diretta, *below the winery on the road to Pontassieve, sells the estate's olive oil and honey as well as its Chianti Rufina.*

Frescobaldi's Tenuta di Pomino lies just outside the village. Here, modern technology works alongside tradition, with the use of temperature-controlled stainless steel fermentation vats, a contrast to the wooden ones previously used during the *mezzadria* (share cropping). Leave the village through the vineyards, the lower slopes to the right mainly for black grapes, the higher slopes on the left for white varieties. The highest of all is Il Benefizio, where Chardonnay grapes grow at the dizzy altitude of 700m (2300ft).

At Borselli, take the road to the right toward the Arno Valley. About half-way down the hill Frescobaldi's magnificent flagship estate, Castello di Nipozzano, dominates this part of the Rufina zone. Its vineyards, up to 400m (1300ft) above sea level, enjoy fine, open southerly exposures, and produce some of the zone's greatest wines: Castello di Nipozzano, a Chianti Rufina Riserva made only in the finest years; Montesodi, a single vineyard Cru Chianti Rufina; and Mormoreto, a super-Tuscan Cabernet Sauvignon. The oldest part of the castle itself dates back to about AD 1000. Like Selvapiana, however, it too was virtually destroyed in World War Two.

From Nipozzano, descend to the Arno Valley, and from there either return to Pontassieve, or turn south to San' Ellero, climbing steeply by way of Donnini and Tosi to visit the imposing 11th-century Abbey of Vallombrosa.

Chianti Rufina and Pomino Fact File

In contrast to the vast and more visited Chianti Classico zone, tiny Chianti Rufina and Pomino are quieter and tourist facilities are thinner on the ground.

Information

In summer, Pontassieve runs an information office (opposite the Ristorante Girarrosto). In addition, there are two options in Florence (see p.13).
APT
Via Manzoni 16, 50100 Florence. Tel 055/23320; fax 055/2346284.

Consorzio Chianti Rufina
Lungarno Corsini 4, 50123 Florence. Tel 055/212333; fax 055/210271.

Museo della Vite e del Vino
Villa Poggio Reale, Via Piave 5 50068 Rufina FI. Tel 055/ 8396111.
Wine museum currently being refurbished as the information centre for the Rufina wine zone. Will also house an *enoteca*.

Markets

Dicomano – Saturday
Pélago – Thursday
Pontassieve – Wednesday
Rufina – Saturday

Festivals and Events

Wines from Chianti and Valdisieve are celebrated in Pontassieve by the *Toscanello d'oro* in the third week of May – an award is given to the best wine in each category. In Rufina, the *Bacco Artigiano* festival during the last week of September is a celebration of wines and local handicrafts.

Where to Buy Wine

The Rufina zone does not offer many wine-buying opportunities apart from at the wine estates. The *enoteca* in Villa Poggio Reale should address this problem when operational.
Enoteca Puliti
Viale Duca della Vittoria 11, 50068 Rufina FI.
Silvano Puliti's general store is at present the best source for the wines of Rufina and Pomino.

Trebbiano and Malvasia grapes dry for Vin Santo at Selvapiana. Wine is femented and aged in the caratelli.

Where to Stay and Eat

Osteria La Casellina (R)
Loc. Montebonello, 50060 Pontassieve FI. Tel 055/ 8397580; fax 055/8396213. (L)(L)
In summer, dine at outdoor tables amid the vineyards above Montebonello; traditional and innovative dishes, plus the best wine list in the zone.

Ristorante Girarrosto (R)
Via Garibaldi 27, 50065 Pontassieve FI. Tel 055/ 8368048. (L)(L)
Winter or summer there is always a blazing wood fire and spits loaded with meats (hence the name). You can eat here or buy for a picnic.

Hotel Moderno (H)
Via Londra 5, 50065 Pontassieve FI. Tel 055/8315541; fax 055/ 8369285. (L)(L)
Modern and comfortable, with all the essential amenities, although lacking in atmosphere.

Villa Pitiana (H)(R)
Via Provinciale per Tosi 7, 50060 Donnini FI. Tel 055/ 860259; fax 055/860326. (L)(L)(L)
Renaissance-inspired villa, parts of which date back to the 13th

century. Rooms and mini-apartments in the villa itself, as well as *agriturismo*. The restaurant, which serves meals in the garden in good weather, is one of the finest in the area and offers outstanding service and wines. Swimming pool.

Hotel-Ristorante La Porcinaia (H)(R)
50060 Tosi FI. Tel 055/704433. (L)(L)
Small, friendly hotel-restaurant situated on the road to Vallombrosa. The speciality of the restaurant is mushrooms. Swimming pool.

Locanda Osteria Lo Spiedo (H)(R)
Via Casentinese 229-231, 50060 Borselli FI. Tel 055/8321688; fax 055/8321740. (L)
Family-run *osteria* noted for authentic Tuscan cooking, especially homemade pasta, *funghi porcini* and grilled meats. Outdoor tables. Simple accommodation.

Agriturismo

Fattoria di Basciano
Viale Duca della Vittoria 159, 50068 Rufina FI. Tel 055/ 8397034; fax 055/8399250.
Beautifully restored medieval tower. Apartments sleep four.

Tenuta di Bossi
Via dello Stracchino 32, 50065 Pontassieve FI. Tel 055/ 8317830; fax 055/8364008.
One of the zone's up-and-coming wine estates, Tenuta di Bossi has a number of well-restored stone houses around the 15th-century villa.

Tenuta di Petrognano
Via di Petrognano 40, Loc. Petrognano, 50060 Rufina FI. Tel 055/8318812.
Tastefully decorated apartments on this fine Pomino wine estate, plus the Locanda Praticino where rooms can be rented by the night. The restaurant of the Locanda (which is open to residents only) serves good, simple *cucina casalinga*.

Wines and Wine Villages

The top wine estates in Chianti Rufina and Pomino may be few and far between, but the countryside here takes on a special character: a timeless patchwork of farm plots and vines which fit seamlessly into an otherwise wild and hilly terrain.

Chianti Rufina DOCG The smallest of the 7 Chianti DOCG sub-zones. It is often known simply as Rufina, which some producers prefer, feeling that the association with Chianti, at least until recently, has somewhat demeaned the zone. It is frequently confused with the Chianti producer Ruffino, whose headquarters are located with the zone at Pontassieve.

Basic Rufina has wild cherry and raspberry flavours, with rustic notes. The wines can be very intense, vibrant and wonderfully perfumed, if a little austere initially. But they are, above all, elegant and remarkably long lived.

The Chianti Rufina DOCG rules regarding grapes varieties were, until recently, more flexible than those of the Classico designation. This meant that the DOCG could cover Rufina's best Sangiovese-based wines (with or without the Riserva designation). There is now a certain lack of glamour surrounding the most celebrated super-Tuscans, which is very much in keeping with the low profile and still largely untapped potential of the zone.

Best producers: Basciano, Bossi, Il Cavaliere, Colognole, FRESCOBALDI *(Nipozzano, Montesodi), Galiga e Vetrice,* SELVAPIANA, *Travignoli.*

Dicomano A thriving, ancient market centre in the very north of the Rufina zone. It has some notable architecture, including partly arcaded streets and a 12th-century church. The Contessa Spaletti's Colognole estate lies between here and the town of Rufina.

Pélago Characterful small town in the south-east corner of the Rufina zone and birthplace

of Renaissance sculptor Lorenzo Ghiberti. The most direct route between Pélago and Pontassieve passes the estate of Travignoli.

Pomino DOC The village that gives its name to the wine zone is situated high up in the Appenine foothills. Its 13th-century Pieve di San Bartolomeo has an impressive interior and contains a splendid terracotta by Luca della Robbia.

Chianti Rufina matures in the bottle in the well-organized cellars of the Selvapiana estate.

The wine zone was originally delimited by a grand-ducal edict in 1716, although the decree included much of what is now the Rufina zone. The contemporary Pomino DOC is centred instead on the Tenuta di Pomino, made famous by the Albizi family and now owned by the Marchesi de' Frescobaldi. This eastern enclave is higher than Rufina. Red grape varieties are planted on sandy calcareous soils just below the village. Whites are found even higher: the Cru Il Benefizio is planted at 700m (2300ft), though the zone extends over altitudes of 800–900m (2600–3000ft) toward Consuma.

The Pomino DOC covers red

and white wines: Sangiovese can be complemented by Cabernet Sauvignon, Merlot and Pinot Nero in reds; Chardonnay, Pinot Bianco and Pinot Grigio are used for the whites. The DOC also covers red and white Vin Santo.

Best producers: FRESCOBALDI *(Tenuta di Pomino),* SELVAPIANA *(Petrognano).*

Pontassieve Strategically sited town located at the confluence of the Arno and Sieve rivers and commanding main road and rail links with Emilia-Romagna in the north and Rome in the south. Much damaged in World War Two, it is an important centre for wine commerce, with large merchants producing often inferior generic Chianti. Most notable is the Ruffino operation, owned by the Folonari family, who are based here, but lease or own good quality estates in Chianti Classico, Montalcino and Montepulciano.

Rufina The town that gives its name to the zone. While no architectural gem, it does boast the 16th-century villa Poggio Reale, now a wine museum.

The modern wine zone is an extension of the original area (known as Pomino) delimited by Cosimo III in 1716. The hills create a lower mean temperature than that of Tuscany's other important quality zones, and comprise calcareous soils containing varying amounts of sand or clay. The Sangiovese vines are relatively old and are mainly not the inferior clones planted so widely in Tuscany between 1967 and 1972. The result of these factors is wines that are more structured, with higher acidity and tannin levels than those from the other Chianti zones.

Best producers (super-Tuscan reds): Basciano, Bossi, FRESCOBALDI.

Sieci In the south-west corner of the zone close to Frescobaldi's wine-making facilities and its Remole estate.

The western Chianti Classico, here just south of San Donato in Poggio in the commune of Barbarino Val d'Elsa, generally experiences a warmer but wetter and less-protected mesoclimate than the rest of the zone. The vineyards in the foreground are those of Isole e Olena, one of Tuscany's most dynamic and brilliant estates, lying below the small stone hamlet of Cortine. Notice the partly clay terrain: on steep slopes or after rain, this heavy ground makes work difficult, and special traction is neccessary to negotiate it. On this estate, areas not planted with vines vary from the scrubland of the Macia Morta range to dense, thickly forested woods.

Chianti Classico

Map illustrations: (above) a scene in Greve in Chianti; (centre) the Gallo Nero, the emblem of the Consorzio; (below) the Vignamaggio estate.

TOUR SUMMARY

Each tour follows a circular route starting from a different point within the zone, and one can be easily linked with another.
Tour 1: Northern Chianti Classico Starting from Florence, and heading south into northern Chianti Classico, visiting estates around San Casciano, the market town of Greve in Chianti and Panzano.
Tour 2: Heart of Chianti Storico Starting from Radda in Chianti, and visiting wine estates and castles by way of Gaiole in Chianti and Castelnuovo Berardenga.
Tour 3: South-western Chianti Classico Starting from Siena to explore the southern and western areas of Chianti Classico through Castellina in Chianti, San Donato in Poggio and Vagliagli.

Distance covered
Tour 1 70km (45 miles).
Tour 2 100km (60 miles).
Tour 3 105km (65 miles).

Time needed 7 hours for each tour, not including detours.

Terrain The roads throughout Chianti Classico, with the exception of main arteries, are in poor condition; there are many unpaved roads, which are dusty in dry weather, slippery and muddy in wet.

Hotels Chianti Classico is one of the finest areas in Italy for wine tourism, and there are good hotels at all price ranges; *agriturismo* is also highly developed.

Restaurants There are plenty of good, local *trattorie* serving robust, country food, as well as fine luxury restaurants and rustic farmhouse cuisine on the wine estates.

Chianti Classico is the wine heartland of Tuscany, a swathe of beautiful countryside that served in times past as the battleground in the struggles between Florence and Siena. Indeed, the name is derived from the Lega del Chianti, a defensive alliance between Radda, Gaiole and Castellina formed in the 13th century against the Sienese, with the Gallo Nero (Black Rooster) as its emblem. Today, the Gallo Nero is the symbol of an altogether different organization – the Consorzio del Marchio Storico Chianti Classico, one of the organizations representing the estates of the DOCG zone. The region's reputation, however, has been elevated as much by prestigious and expensive super-Tuscan vini da tavola as those of the DOCG. The super-Tuscans are, for most producers, the pinnacle of quality, and are typically full-bodied, structured and ageworthy, with ripe, concentrated fruit. Chianti Classico ranges from light, supple quaffers to darker, more concentrated and long-lived versions most evident in Riserva.

Chianti Classico is so vast, with over 600 winegrowers within its boundaries, that the zone has been divided into three separate tours.

Tour 1: Northern Chianti Classico

Leave Florence on the S2, the old Roman Via Cassia (the exit for this from the A1 *autostrada* is Firenze Certosa). After passing Florence's old Cistercian monastery, and just beyond the town of Tavarnuzze, the signs proclaim, *Siete nel Mondo del Gallo Nero* – 'You are now in the world of the Black Rooster', the Chianti Classico zone. Just beyond Tavarnuzze, take the right fork to Sant' Andrea in Percussina, where Niccolò Machiavelli lived while writing his famous treatise, *Il Principe* (*The Prince*); there is a small museum here dedicated to the Florentine writer and strategist. The Consorzio del Marchio Storico Chianti Classico is next door (although it is due to move to Radda in Chianti in the year 2000). It is worth stopping to pick up a detailed map of the wine zone – essential for touring on small roads. Nearby is the Conti Serristori winery, part of the Gruppo Italiano Vini (GIV) – Italy's largest winery, making 70 million bottles per year. Its extensive *cantina* can also be visited, beneath the old *osteria* where Machiavelli took his meals.

From Sant' Andrea, continue to San Casciano Val di Pesa, the production headquarters of Tuscany's leading winery, Antinori, which boast numerous estates not only in Chianti Classico (Santa Cristina, Badia a Passignano, Pèppoli), but also in Bolgheri (Tenuta Belvedere) and Montepulciano (La Braccesca). The Antinori family can

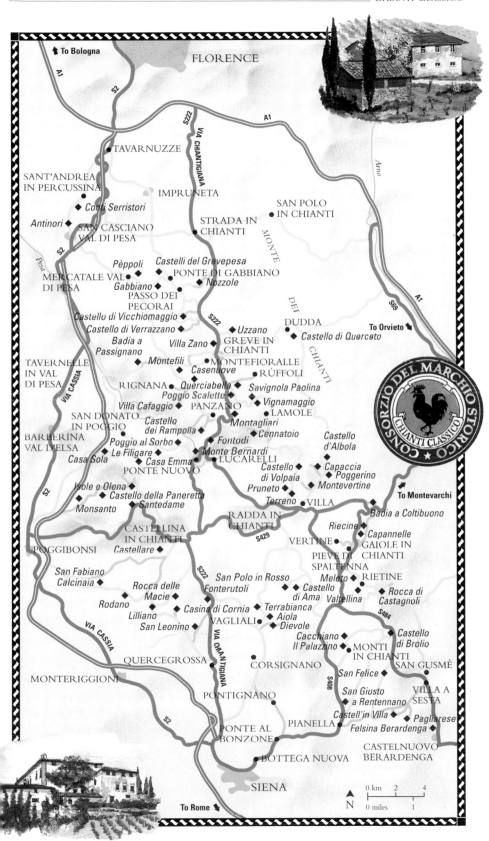

To Bologna

FLORENCE

A1

S2

S222

VIA CHIANTIGIANA

A1

Arno

TAVARNUZZE

SANT'ANDREA
IN PERCUSSINA

IMPRUNETA

SAN POLO
IN CHIANTI

Conti Serristori

STRADA IN
CHIANTI

Antinori

SAN CASCIANO
VAL DI PESA

MONTE

S2

Pesa

Pèppoli

Castelli del Grevepesa

MERCATALE VAL
DI PESA

PONTE DI GABBIANO

Gabbiano

Nozzole

PASSO DEI
PECORAI

DEI

S69

A1

Castello di Vicchiomaggio

S222

DUDDA

To Orvieto

Castello di Verrazzano

Uzzano

Castello di Querceto

Badia a
Passignano

Villa Zano

GREVE IN
CHIANTI

TAVERNELLE
IN VAL
DI PESA

VIA CASSIA

Montefili

MONTEFIORALLE

CHIANTI

Casenuove

RÙFFOLI

RIGNANA

Querciabella

Savignola Paolina

Poggio Scaletto

Vignamaggio

Villa Cafaggio

PANZANO

LAMOLE

SAN DONATO
IN POGGIO

Castello
dei Rampolla

Montagliari

Cennatoio

Castello
d'Albola

BARBERINA
VAL D'ELSA

Poggio al Sorbo

Fontodi

Le Filigare

Monte Bernardi

Casa Sola

Casa Emma

LUCARELLI

PONTE NUOVO

Castello
di Volpaia

Capaccia
Poggerino

Isole e Olena

Pruneto

Montevertine

To Montevarchi

Castello della Paneretta

Terreno

VILLA

Monsanto

Santedame

RADDA IN
CHIANTI

Badia a Coltibuono

CASTELLINA
IN CHIANTI

Riecine

Capannelle

S429

VERTINE

GAIOLE IN

POGGIBONSI

Castellare

PIEVE DI CHIANTI
SPALTENNA

San Fabiano
Calcinaia

S222

San Polo in Rosso

Meleto

RIETINE

Rocca delle
Macie

Fonterutoli

Castello
di Ama

Rocca di
Castagnoli

Rodano

Casina di Cornia

Valtellina

Lilliano

Terrabianca

S484

San Leonino

VAGLIALI

Aiola

VIA CASSIA

Dievole

VIA CHIANTIGIANA

Cacchiano
Il Palazzino

MONTI
IN CHIANTI

Castello
di Brolio

QUERCEGROSSA

CORSIGNANO

SAN GUSMÈ

MONTERIGGIONI

San Felice

PONTIGNANO

S408

San Giusto
a Rentennano

VILLA A
SESTA

S2

Castell'in Villa

Pagliarese

PIANELLA

Felsina Berardenga

PONTE AL
BONZONE

CASTELNUOVO
BERARDENGA

BOTTEGA NUOVA

SIENA

To Rome

0 km   2   4

N

0 miles   1

claim more than 600 years of uninterrupted production, and the winery itself has been in San Casciano for nearly 100 years.

Head to Mercatale Val di Pesa, a quiet village which serves as a market centre for those in the isolated estates that surround it. Continue straight through, following signs to Greve. Antinori's Pèppoli estate is on the left, and just beyond on the right is an impressive fortification with stout watchtowers and crenellations, housing the estate winery of Gabbiano. Just before the main Greve road is the large co-operative Castelli del Grevepesa. Its best wines are from specific sub-zones, and all are available to taste and buy.

Turn right at Ponte di Gabbiano toward Greve. A detour to the right leads to Nozzole, one of Ruffino's leading estates and source of acclaimed Cabernet-based super-Tuscan Il Pareto. Just past Passo dei Pecorai, take the left fork that leads to Castello di Vicchiomaggio, a Renaissance castle majestically sited on a strategic hilltop. At the entrance to the English-owned estate is a welcoming *vendita diretta*: try the fascinating La Prima, an intensely concentrated Chianti Classico made from the oldest vines on the estate, some of them still trained up trees in the old method of cultivation.

Rejoin the Via Chiantigiana (S222) that follows the Greve Valley to Greve in Chianti itself, passing a long dirt drive on the right leading to Castello di Verrazzano, noted for its long-lived traditional Riserva and, further on, another to Uzzano on the left, whose beautiful Italianate formal gardens are a great spot for a picnic (the estate can supply food and wine). Just north of the town, down a little road to the right, is Villa Zano, a large estate and source of grapes for many of Ruffino's wines.

Greve in Chianti is one of the most important market towns in Chianti Classico, dominated by its fine, irregular 17th-century piazza. The Enoteca del Gallo Nero, just off the market square, is one of the best wine shops in Chianti Classico, but don't miss the Antica Macelleria Falorni, one of the zone's finest producers of traditional *salumi*.

Wine estates radiate in all directions from Greve. A detour on the road east to Dudda leads to Castello di Querceto, once under the imperial jurisdiction of the Holy Roman Emperor Frederick II, which dominates the strategic route between the Arno Valley and Greve. Try any of the three fine super-Tuscans, although the Chianti Classico Riserva Il Picchio can sometimes be even better. The estate also provides snacks or meals by prior arrangement.

Heading west out of Greve, the road leads to the small fortified hill hamlet of Montefioralle, beautifully restored and still almost wholly located within its intact medieval walls. Beyond Montefioralle, little now remains of the Montefili castle, destroyed in 1260 by the Ghibellines, but the lands around the site are still known as the Vecchie

In Tuscany, wine estates often occupy high, isolated hilltops, like Castello di Verrazzano (in the foreground) and Castello di Vichiomaggio (beyond).

Terre di Montefili. Today these vine-covered hills belong to the wine estate of the same name, noted for its outstanding super-Tuscans Anfiteatro Riserva and Bruno di Rocca, as well as Chianti Classico.

Returning to Greve, head south on the S222, then look for a turning to the left to Lamole, a dramatic, unpaved pass that eventually leads to Radda in Chianti, by way of Castello di Volpaia and Terreno (see Tour 2). Off to the left, near the little hamlet of Rùffoli, is Querciabella, one of Greve's outstanding estates, noted for its Chianti Classico, super-Tuscan Camartina, a wine of great depth and finesse, and Pinot Bianco-based Bâtard – probably Tuscany's best white. Nearby is the rising star Poggio Scalette, whose Il Carbonaione is already one of the purest expressions of Sangiovese yet made. This is, after all, the personal venture of Vittorio Fiore, the man who has a hand in many of Tuscany's finest wines.

Further on, as the cypress-lined road begins to climb, the soil is predominantly *galestro*. Savignola Paolina, to the left, is a reliable small producer of characterful Chianti Classico. The pink 15th-century villa of Vignamaggio, another leading estate, is famous as the birthplace of Mona Lisa de'Gherardini, immortalized in Leonardo da Vinci's masterpiece; more recently, the estate was the setting for the film *Much Ado About Nothing*. Its most consistently impressive wines are fine Chianti Classico Riserva and the predominantly Sangiovese Gherardino.

Carry on over the high hills to Lamole, stopping off in the hamlet for a coffee, or a glass of wine and a sandwich. Beyond Lamole, a road to the right descends to Panzano in Chianti. About half way down on the left is Cennatoio, a welcoming estate (in spite of its imposing gates) and the source of good-quality wines, especially the concentrated pure Sangiovese Etrusco.

The hilltop village of Panzano, a small *frazione* of the Greve sub-zone, is a good place to stock up for vineyard picnics: the Antica Macelleria Cecchini is a fascinating old shop producing excellent *salumi*, while the Panificio Cennini is the source of delicious Tuscan breads and *biscotti*. The town is surrounded by quality wine estates. To the south is Fontodi, source of the now classic super-Tuscan Flaccianello della Pieve, an outstanding barrique-aged pure Sangiovese. Just beyond is the tiny new winery of Monte Bernardi – the wines are expensive but have quickly acquired a cult following. North-east of the town, Giovanni Cappelli's Montagliari estate offers good, characterful wines, as well as local food in its reliable farmhouse *trattoria*.

Continue through Panzano heading north back to Mercatale. Castello dei Rampolla, down a road to the left just outside Panzano leading to the hamlet of Santa Lucia in

Vineyards surround the little hamlet of Montefiorale, near the wine town of Greve in Chianti.

Faulle, has been in the Di Napoli family since 1739, and is one of the most dynamic estates in Chianti Classico. Its wines are wholly singular and of the highest quality, notably the legendary Sammarco (Cabernet Sauvignon with a little Sangiovese aged in barrique), as well as concentrated and elegant Chianti Classico. Further north, another road to the left just past Casenuove leads to Villa Cafaggio, another of Panzano's consistently high-quality estates.

Further on still, yet another left turn leads to the impressive fortified Vallombrosan monastery of Badia a Passignano, a wealthy order founded in 1049 which once controlled extensive vineyard holdings around the fortified village. The immense vaulted cellars below the abbey are impressive, and store Antinori's Tignanello, one of Tuscany's first and still one of its greatest super-Tuscans, produced from Sangiovese with the addition of about 20 per cent Cabernet Sauvignon, and Solaia, a richly intense Cabernet Sauvignon with a little Cabernet Franc and Sangiovese. Vineyards surrounding the abbey have been replanted in recent years to produce Antinori's Badia a Passignano Chianti Classico. Although it is normally not possible to visit the wine cellars, there is an adjoining shop stocking the full range of Antinori wines. From here, return to Florence or join one of the other tours.

Tour 2: Heart of Chianti Storico

The Chianti Storico corresponds to the area formed by the Lega del Chianti in the 13th century. It was only in 1932 that the zone expanded beyond this original territory to something like its present dimensions to become the Chianti Classico wine zone. The tour starts in Radda in Chianti, a small but typical fortified Chianti town, with municipal buildings, private palaces and characterful narrow lanes within the medieval Rocca. The Consorzio is in the process of moving its headquarters here to the Santa Maria in Prato, a 16th-century Franciscan convent. This historic edifice will serve as a cultural centre, including wine and art museums, and should be complete by the year 2000. The Vignavecchia estate has an outlet in Radda, while the Gastronomia Porciatti is a fine source of picnic provisions.

Leave Radda on the road to Gaiole, then immediately find the turning to Villa and head north toward the Parco di Cavriglia. Sergio Manetti's Montevertine, located soon to the left, is one of the great wine estates of Chianti Classico and an early pioneer of super-Tuscan wines, with its now classic Pergole Torte, a hugely concentrated pure Sangiovese normally aged for about 6–8 months in new barriques. Manetti has established a museum of farm implements, although opportunities for visiting the estate itself are limited.

Castello dei Rampolla, seen here from the vineyard of Fontodi, is situated in the Conca d'Oro (Golden Shell) of Panzano, and is an outstanding estate.

Further up this dramatic valley is the Poggerino winery, where young Piero Lanza maintains quality first and foremost in his Chianti Classico. Continue a little further up the valley, then take courage and make your way up the rough track on the left to a still only partially restored medieval hamlet and the tiny Capaccia estate. This is one of the most welcoming in the zone, and provided someone is on hand to receive you (weekends are best when Giampaolo Pacini and his family are 'at home'), it is possible to taste and purchase wines. Enologist Vittorio Fiore's magic touch is evident here, especially in pure Sangiovese thoroughbred Querciagrande, one of the zone's earliest – and finest – super-Tuscans.

The top of the valley is dominated by the villa and winery of Castello d'Albola, part of the family-owned house of Zonin, which is better known for its extensive and consistent range of bulk wines from the Veneto and elsewhere.

More important wine estates lie on the hills to the west of this range. To reach them, return to Radda, then find the road that leads across to Panzano via Lucarelli. A few kilometres out of Radda, turn right to Volpaia and right again at the next fork, passing Terreno on the way, source of excellent Chianti Classico and also one of the most welcoming places to stay. More excellent Chianti can be had at the neighbouring estate of Pruneto.

The hamlet of Volpaia, further up the road, is built within the walls of its 12th-century castle on a high strategic point looking across to Radda. This is a magnificent place from which to enjoy views or else park in the piazza and head up to the woods above for fine walks or a picnic. Castello di Volpaia is one of the area's leading wine producers, helped by enologist Maurizio Castelli. All the wines exhibit an uncommon refinement, from Chianti Classico through super-Tuscans to Vin Santo. The shop in the piazza sells the estate's wines, olive oil, vinegar and honey, while the bar/shop known as La Bottega serves excellent local food, in particular exquisite hand-made ravioli.

Return to Radda, this time taking the road to Gaiole. After about 4km (2½ miles) look for a turning left to Badia a Coltibuono, a fascinating collection of stone buildings comprising the Vallombrosan monastery and abbey, founded in 1058 and extended in the 15th and 18th centuries. The cellars beneath the abbey are still in use for the estate's consistently high-quality range of wines, though the working *cantina*, a new purpose-built winery, is located near the main vineyard holdings at Monti in Chianti. There is also an excellent restaurant on the estate serving traditional food in a rustic setting.

From Badia a Coltibuono, continue to the pleasant market town of Gaiole in Chianti, stopping en route at

Radda in Chianti is one of the major wine towns of Chianti Classico, and like all the ancient fortified settlements in the region, occupies a commanding hilltop position.

Riecine, where Englishman John Dunkley makes refined Chianti Classico, particularly the Riserva, and sometimes exceptional super-Tuscan La Gioia. A little further on, the Capannelle estate produces a number of super-Tuscans, the most notable being Capannelle Rosso aged in barrique.

Gaiole lies at the foot of a pass that connects the Monti del Chianti with the Arno Valley. Sited on the lowlands, it never had its own fortifications or watchtowers, yet still formed an integral part of the Lega del Chianti military alliance. The Pieve di Spaltenna, a fortified hill complex just above Gaiole, afforded the town some protection: a walled castle (now a hotel) and ancient church whose oldest part dates back to 1003. Carry on past Spaltenna to visit the fine, still unspoiled and little-visited stone hamlet of Vertine.

Head south from Gaiole on the road to Siena, but just a couple of kilometres out of town, look for a turning to the left to Rietine and Castagnoli. Castello di Meleto is a stout, 12th-century military fortress; transformed into a private villa in the 18th century, it has a private theatre that is still in use. The wines that bear the castle's name are produced by the Storiche Cantine di Radda co-operative. Cristoph Schneider continues to lever the Valtellina estate, located in the small hamlet of Rietine, ever higher. Both Chianti Classico and Sangiovese-Cabernet super-Tuscan Convivio are elegant and structured. Continue through the vineyards to Castagnoli, quiet, little visited, with stone-paved streets and a stout medieval fortress. The Rocca di Castagnoli winery may be located within the walls of the ancient hamlet but the *cantina* of this reinvigorated estate is modern and up to date, best reflected in Cabernet Buriano and Sangiovese-Cabernet Stielle. There is a good, friendly *osteria*, L'Alto Chianti, just outside Castagnoli.

The lively market town of Gaiole in Chianti gives its name to a commune with several high-quality estates.

From Castagnoli, follow the road around to San Martino al Vento, then turn left to join the main road that leads to Castelnuovo Berardenga. The next important monument a few kilometres further on is the massive Castello di Brolio, which has belonged to the Ricasoli family since the 12th century. It was Barone Bettino Ricasoli, dubbed the 'Iron Baron' when he became Prime Minister of Italy, who devised a 'recipe' for Chianti in the mid-19th century, which until recently remained the basis for the wines. The Ricasoli winery, an immense complex located below the castle, is now back in the hands of the family under the leadership of Barone Francesco Ricasoli, whose new team includes enologist Carlo Ferrini. Its revival should be exciting to follow; the finest wines, which bear the Castello di Brolio label, have already demonstrated considerable improvement in quality.

The south-eastern corner of Chianti Classico enjoys a warm mesoclimate, reflected in the warmer, fleshier styles

of wine produced here. Leading estates along this stretch include San Felice, which produces good Chianti Classico,
though the Riserva Poggio Rosso and Sangiovese-
Cabernet Vigorello are the most exceptional; and, just outside Castelnuovo Berardenga, the magnificent Felsina
Berardenga, source of immensely ripe and powerful yet
balanced Chianti Classico as well as fine, oak-influenced
super-Tuscan Fontalloro.

The magnificent and imposing Castello di Brolio is one of many ancient castles in Chianti Classico.

Drop by to visit Castelnuovo Berardenga, or return toward Gaiole, and after about 2km (1 mile) take the left
turn to Pianella. This unpaved road leads first to Pagliarese
off to the left, then to the renowned Castell'in Villa, which
not only produces outstandingly rich, intense yet elegant
wines (recently assisted by Giacomo Tachis, the wine-
making guru who established Tignanello), but also houses
a superb restaurant.

At Pianella, turn right to Gaiole and after about 1km
(½ mile), right again to the outstanding estate of San Giusto
a Rentennano, in ancient times a monastery but transformed into a villa in the 15th century. Back on the S408,
another turning to the right (to Monti in Chianti) leads to
the tiny but highly rated Il Palazzino and Cacchiano estates.
The latter, a historic monument dating from 1203, is a long-
standing traditional estate noted for its big, hearty if slightly
four-square Chiantis.

Continuing toward Gaiole, take the left fork to the fortified hamlet of Ama. The castle was destroyed in the 15th
century, its ruins transformed into the villa of Castello di
Ama some centuries later. Today, this is one of the most
prestigious estates in the zone, producing wines from well-
sited single vineyards such as Bellavista and La Casuccia.

On from Ama, a track on the left leads to San Polo in Rosso, the old agricultural holding transformed today into a modern wine estate. Under the influence of Maurizio Castelli, it produces a rounded, stylish Chianti Classico and super-Tuscan Cetinaia. From here, it is only a short drive back to Radda, while turning to the left leads to Castellina.

Tour 3: South-western Chianti Classico

This corner of the Classico zone is less typical, perhaps, than the rest, with a series of ridges running from east to west which makes the area difficult to negotiate by road. This is more than compensated for by the splendid views across the open country to San Gimignano and beyond.

From Siena, head north on the S222 and, just beyond Quercegrossa, turn left to San Leonino, a hamlet with a modern winery of the same name. Continue through the majestic wine country, passing the small estate of Cascina di Cornia, source of characterful organic wines and fine ceramics. The Lilliano estate is located in an impressive villa, with wines to match, in the centre of the small village which once comprised lands belonging to Badia a Coltibuono. A road to the right leads to Rocca delle Macie, the large wine estate of film maker Italo Zingarelli of spaghetti western fame.

Continue toward Poggibonsi to visit Rodano and San Fabiano Calcinaia, then turn back to Castellina in Chianti. Just before the town is Castellare, whose vineyards surround the monastery of San Nicolò, after which the estate's individual super-Tuscan, I Sodi di San Nicolò, is named.

The medieval Rocca, or fortress, was essential for the defence of Castellina in Chianti, one of the three members of the Lega del Chianti.

Castellina in Chianti is located on a commanding spur of land between the Arbia and Elsa valleys. It is dominated by its medieval Rocca, or fortress, that gives the walled town its name of 'little castle'. Long at the forefront of Florentine defences, today Castellina is one of the most pleasant and peaceful centres in the zone, with several good *enoteche*.

Head north toward San Donato in Poggio, passing over the high Macia Morta ridge, covered with scrubland rather than vines. A left turn leads to Ruffino's Santedame estate, where Chianti Classico is always at least good. As the road descends, look for another left turn to Isola e Olena. Paolo De Marchi's dynamic estate, at the end of an olive-tree-lined drive, is the source of wines of the highest class, notably intense and full-bodied Chianti Classico, and the highly acclaimed super-Tuscan Sangiovese Cepparello, named after a stream that runs through the property. Further on is the large, imposing 15th-century Castello della Paneretta, the centre of a large agricultural estate. The impressive wines here include a distinctive super-Tuscan, Terrine, unusual in combining a high percentage of Canaiolo with Sangiovese.

Not far beyond, on the westernmost fringe of the Classico zone, is the second great estate of the commune of Barberino Val d'Elsa, Monsanto. Located on the end of a high bluff overlooking the Elsa Valley, its warm, sheltered mesoclimate and calcareous *galestro* terrain, most notably on the famous Il Poggio site, result in immensely long-lived wines of enormous extract and ripeness. The underground cellars of Monsanto include a beautiful stone gallery, and have room for 800 barriques and 350,000 bottles.

Continue toward Poggibonsi, then after about 2km (1 mile), look for a turning to the right that leads back to San Donato, passing on the way two good small producers, Casa Sola and, to the right along the main road, Casa Emma. To the north, the small, quiet stone hamlet of San Donato in Poggio has an informal *trattoria*, La Toppa, which makes a good stop for a bite to eat.

Leaving San Donato on the road that returns to Castellina, next find the turning to the left to Piazza. Wine estates on this stretch include Le Filigare and Poggio al Sorbo, a 16th-century villa constructed on the site of an important medieval military tower. After Piazza, a small hamlet with a fine *osteria*, head due south at Ponte Nuovo to return to Castellina. Pass through the town, heading back toward Siena. After 4km (2½ miles) or so is the hamlet of Fonterutoli, home to the noble Mazzei family since 1435. Their Castello di Fonterutoli wines rate among Castellina's most brilliant, and can be tasted and purchased in the Osteria di Fonterutoli.

Turn back toward Castellina, taking the first right, and after about 5km (3 miles) turn left to Radda (see Tour 2). After passing through Vagliagli, perhaps stopping off at the friendly wine bar, on the right is Aiola, centred on the impressive military fortification of the Castello dell'Aiola, whose well-organized tasting room and cellars are worth a visit. A little further on the left is Terrabianca, also offering tastings and direct sales. These are modern, stylish wines; Sangiovese-Cabernet Campaccio (also in a Riserva version) is the top wine.

Turn back toward Siena, taking the next left for the final estate of the tour – Dievole, a self-sufficient agricultural community that is the personal fiefdom of Mario Schwenn, a young Swiss winemaker with singular character and ideas. Fascinating tours of the estate and winery begin in the chapel, with a glass of wine in hand.

Finally, continue south past Corsignano, then find a fork left to the Certosa di Pontignano, a Cistercian monastery founded in 1343. It is worth stopping here to wander through its vast and airy cloisters, or perhaps to enjoy a picnic. From here, return to Siena by way of Ponte al Bozzone and Bottega Nuova.

The little village of Fonterutoli, near Castellina in Chianti, is home to Castello di Fonterutoli, one of the best estates of the sub-zone.

Chianti Classico Fact File

The Chianti Classico region is the most welcoming of all Tuscany's wine zones. Easily reached from Florence or Siena, the wine villages of Castellina and Radda make ideal bases for those who prefer the countryside to the city. There are hotels and restaurants throughout the region to suit all pockets, as well as superb *agriturismo*.

Information

Pro Loco
Via B. Ricasoli 50, 53013 Gaiole in Chianti SI. Tel 0577/749411.

Pro Loco
Piazza Ferrucci 1, 53017 Radda in Chianti SI. Tel 0577/738494.

Ufficio Cultura
Comune di Greve in Chianti, Piazza Matteotti 8, 50022 Greve in Chianti FI. Tel 055/8545219.

Consorzio del Marchio Storico Chianti Classico
Via Scopeti 155, Loc. S. Andrea in Percussina, 50026 San Casciano Val di Pesa FI. Tel 055/8228245; fax 055/8228173. Helpful wine information and a good detailed map showing all the wineries of the zone. Due to relocate to Radda in Chianti in the year 2000.

Wine Experiences in Tuscany
Compagnia dei Vignaioli, 53017 Radda in Chianti. Tel & fax 0577/738385.
Wine and gastronomy tours arranged to order, including visits to wine estates, group tastings, wine seminars and cookery courses.

Markets

Castellina in Chianti – Saturday
Gaiole in Chianti – 2nd Monday of each month
Greve in Chianti – Saturday
Impruneta – Saturday
Panzano in Chianti – Sunday
Radda in Chianti – 4th Monday afternoon of each month
San Casciano Val di Pesa – Monday
San Donato in Poggio – Friday
San Polo in Chianti – Thursday
Strada in Chianti – Monday

Festivals and Events

Sagre o feste della vendemmia o dell'uva – wine and harvest festivals – take place throughout the wine country, mainly in September. Three such notable festivals, all at the end of the month, are at Impruneta, San Casciano Val di Pesa and Mercatale Val di Pesa. The most important of the zone's wine celebrations is the *Rassegna del Chianti Classico,* which occurs in mid-September in Greve in Chianti. It is a chance for winegrowers to display the fruits of their efforts,

Shopping is transported in the old-fashioned way, here in the old town of Radda in Chianti.

as well as for those from outlying districts and hamlets to get together and exchange news and information.

Enoteche and Bars

There are scores of opportunities for tasting and purchasing wine in the Chianti Classico zone. Virtually every town and hamlet has its outlet selling wines, and there is no shortage of congenial bars where good wines can be sampled.

Bottega di Badia a Passignano
Loc. Badia a Passignano, 50020 Sambuca Val di Pesa FI.
Located in an ancient presshouse beside the Vallombrosan abbey, this shop offers the full range of Antinori's wines. There is also an interesting display of barrels and barriques.

Enoteca Baldi
Piazza Bucciarelli 25, 50020 Panzano in Chianti FI.
Recently established *enoteca,* which is a good place to enjoy wines together with snacks or local food. There is an intelligent and well-kept selection available by the glass, but wines can also be purchased by the bottle or case.

La Cantinetta del Chianti
Via F. Ferrucci 20, 53013 Gaiole in Chianti SI. Tel & fax 0577/749125.
Attractive display of some of the finest wines from the whole of the Chianti Classico zone – Castello di Ama, Fontodi, Querciabella, Isole e Olena, Castello dei Rampolla, Podere Capaccia, Giorgio Regni and others. Roberto Maestrini offers sound advice.

Enoteca del Chianti Classico
Via G Verrazzano 8–10, 50020 Panzano in Chianti FI.
This dark den is a warren of bottle-laden shelves from leading estates throughout the Chianti Classico zone as well as the rest of Tuscany. There is a small selection of food specialities, which includes extra virgin olive oil, wonderful aromatic vinegars and honey.

Bar-Enoteca Dante Alighieri
Piazza Dante Alighieri, 53017 Radda in Chianti SI.
Typical neighbourhood bar which has recently been restored, but remains as popular and friendly as ever. Excellent selection of wines available by the glass, with snacks, plus a good selection of bottles to buy at fair prices.

Enoteca del Gallo Nero
Piazzetta S. Croce 8, 50022
Greve in Chianti FI.
Probably the best and most
comprehensive *enoteca* in the
zone and the only one that
exhibits wines from all the
commercial producers of Chianti
Classico. Large, well-displayed
selection includes not only
Chianti, but also all the finest
Tuscan wines

La Cantina di Vagliagli
Via del Sergente 6, 53010
Vagliagli SI.
Stylish wine bar, in the centre of
the small village, which stays
open late and is popular with the
local youth. Wines by the glass
or bottle together with simple
pasta and pizza.

Bottega del Vino
Via della Rocca 1, 53011
Castellina in Chianti SI.
Small select display of some of
the finest Tuscan wines, not just
Chianti Classico, but also
Brunello, Vino Nobile,
Vernaccia di San Gimignano and
super-Tuscans.

Where to Stay and Eat
Casali dell'Aiola Ⓗ
Fattoria dell'Aiola, Strada
Provinciale di Vagliagli 54,
53010 Vagliagli SI Tel & fax
0577/322797. Ⓛ
Small, nicely restored and
tranquil hotel on a wine estate in
the midst of the vineyards. Seven
double rooms and one suite, all
with private facilities.

L'Alto Chianti Ⓡ
Loc. Castagnoli, 53013 Gaiole in
Chianti SI. Tel 0577/731008. Ⓛ
Small, friendly *trattoria* in a
restored attic hayloft, serving
good, seasonal dishes with a
menu that changes every month.
Come here for full meals, or just
for a drink or a snack. The wine
list is well-chosen as well as
reasonably priced.

Ristorante Badia a Coltibuono Ⓡ
Loc. Badia a Coltibuono, 53013
Gaiole in Chianti SI. Tel 0577/
749031. Ⓛ Ⓛ
This rustic/elegant restaurant on

The Enoteca del Gallo Nero has a great selection of wines and local produce.

the famous wine estate serves
both traditional and creative
dishes, as well as recipes devised
by Lorenza de'Medici. In the
afternoon, there are simpler
snacks available.

Hotel Belvedere di San Leonino Ⓗ
Loc. San Leonino, 53011
Castellina in Chianti SI. Tel
0577/740887; fax 0577/740924.
Ⓛ Ⓛ
Restored 15th-century country
hotel with panoramic views and
swimming pool.

Relais Borgo San Felice Ⓗ Ⓡ
Loc. San Felice, 53019
Castelnuovo Berardenga SI. Tel
0577/359260; fax 0577/359089.
Ⓛ Ⓛ Ⓛ
This luxury hotel/restaurant
complex, set in a beautiful
restored medieval hamlet, is part
of the select Relais & Châteaux
group. The restaurant serves
mainly seasonal, locally inspired
meals in an elegant dining room
or, in fine weather, on a terrace
overlooking the vineyards. The
wines of the San Felice estate are
considered among the finest in the
Chianti Classico zone.

La Bottega Ⓡ
Piazza della Torre 2, Loc.
Volpaia, 53017 Radda in Chianti
SI. Tel 0577/738001. Ⓛ
It is advisable to book a table at
this simple tavern/shop in
Volpaia's square to enjoy
sensational homemade ravioli,
own-produced *salumi*, and the
wines of Castello di Volpaia.

Ristorante Castell'in Villa Ⓡ
Loc. Castell'in Villa, 53019
Castelnuovo Berardenga SI. Tel
0577/359356. Ⓛ Ⓛ
This stylish, futuristic dining
room, created out of this well-
known wine estate's *vecchia
cantina* and hung with modern
paintings, reflects its dynamic
mix of the traditional and the
ultra-modern. Cuisine is
excellent and ranges beyond the
strictly local to embrace broader
elements of the Mediterranean
diet, accompanied, of course, by
the fine Castell'in Villa wines.

Il Cenobio a Vignamaggio Ⓗ
Loc. Vignamaggio, 50022 Greve
in Chianti FI. Tel 055/8544840;
fax 055/8544468. Ⓛ Ⓛ
Small, comfortable private hotel
above Greve on the
Vignamaggio wine estate where
da Vinci's model Mona Lisa was
born. Minimum stay 2 nights.

Osteria di Fonterutoli Ⓡ
Loc. Fonterutoli, 53011
Castellina in Chianti SI. Tel
0577/740212. Ⓛ
Popular *osteria* in the medieval
hamlet of Fonterutoli. Dishes are
strictly *cucina casalinga*,
accompanied by the fine wines
of this aristocratic estate. The
osteria is also the estate's direct
sales outlet, and wines can be
sampled by the glass.

Albergo-Ristorante Giovanni da Verrazzano Ⓗ Ⓡ
Piazza Matteotti 28, 50022
Greve in Chianti FI. Tel 055/
853189. Ⓛ Ⓛ

Popular traditional hotel/ restaurant in the old market square of Greve, serving typical Tuscan food, together with a wide selection of Chianti Classico wines. The hotel boasts some pleasant rooms overlooking the square.

Taverna del Guerrino Ⓡ
Castello di Montefioralle, 50022 Greve in Chianti FI. Tel 055/853106. Ⓛ
Come to this *taverna* in the steep, cobbled fortified hamlet above Greve to enjoy spectacular views of the Tuscan countryside, as well as simple, homely food such as *ribollita* and grilled meats, and good own-produced Chianti Classico. Open Thursday to Saturday.

Trattoria del Montagliari Ⓡ
Via di Montagliari, 50020 Panzano FI. Tel 055/852014; fax 055/852804. ⓁⓁ
Popular wayside *trattoria*, located between Panzano and Greve, which forms part of the Montagliari wine estate. Good, well-prepared Tuscan food in a relaxed rustic atmosphere – served at outdoor tables in summer.

Bottega del Moro Ⓡ
Piazza Trieste 14r, 50022 Greve in Chianti FI. Tel 055/853753. Ⓛ
Popular and friendly *trattoria* serving both homecooked and innovative food. There is a discreet selection of the best local wines as well as some good whites from Friuli.

Albergaccio Niccolò Macchiavelli Ⓡ
Loc. S. Andrea in Percussina, 50026 San Casciano Val di Pesa FI. Tel 055/828471. ⓁⓁ
This historic *osteria* deserves a visit, not particularly for its cooking, which is adequate, but for its atmosphere and history: it seems to be little changed since the time when the writer Niccolò Macchiavelli used to take his meals here. Ask to visit the extensive underground cellars where wines are still made and aged.

Cantinetta del Nonno Ⓡ
Via IV Novembre 18, 50026 San Casciano Val di Pesa FI. Tel 055/820570. Ⓛ
Stop here for a quick snack and a glass of wine at the bar, good traditional meals in the *osteria*, or *panini* to be made for a picnic in the vineyards.

Ristorante de Padellina Ⓡ
Via Corso del Popolo 54, 50027 Strada in Chianti FI. Tel 055/85388. ⓁⓁ
A reliable bet for authentically prepared *bistecca alla fiorentina*, served with a good selection of

Chianti Classico's many bars provide ideal spots to relax after a day's touring.

Chianti Classico and super-Tuscan wines.

Osteria alla Piazza ⒽⓇ
Loc. La Piazza, 53011 Castellina in Chianti SI. Tel 0577/733580. ⓁⓁ
Friendly local *osteria* with a reputation for serving some of the finest traditional dishes in Chianti, most notably *bistecca alla fiorentina*, prepared with care and precision. Excellent wine list. Rooms available.

La Cantinetta di Rignana Ⓡ
Via Rignana 13, Loc. Rignana, 50022 Greve in Chianti FI. Tel 055/852601. Ⓛ
Signposted down a track located roughly between Badia a Passignano and Panzano, this rustic country restaurant serves good seasonal food and meat cooked over a wood fire. The wines come from the Fattoria di Rignana.

Hotel Salivolpi Ⓗ
Via Fiorentina, 53011 Castellina in Chianti SI. Tel 0577/740484; fax 0577/740998. ⓁⓁ
This comfortable, restored country house outside Castellina on the road to San Donato makes an excellent base for touring the wine country. Swimming pool.

Il Salotto del Chianti Ⓡ
Via Sonnino 92, Loc. Mercatale Val di Pesa, 50026 San Casciano Val di Pesa FI. Tel 055/8218016. ⓁⓁ
Small, highly regarded restaurant (open evenings only) serving creative dishes based on fresh seasonal ingredients, and with one of the best wine lists in the Chianti Classico.

Trattoria San Regolo Ⓡ
Loc. San Regolo 33, 53013 Gaiole in Chianti SI. Tel 0577/747136. Ⓛ
Simple *trattoria* near the Castello di Brolio noted for its faithfully traditional food, especially *girarrosti* (spit-roasted meat).

Castello di Spaltenna ⒽⓇ
Loc. Spaltenna, 53013 Gaiole in Chianti SI. Tel 0577/749483; fax 0577/749269. ⓁⓁⓁ
Ancient fortified monastery, now an expensive luxury hotel/ restaurant in the wine hills above Gaiole. In summer elegant meals are served in the shaded stone cloisters, while there is a bar/ *enoteca* in the vaulted wine cellars. Swimming pool.

Palazzo Squarcialupi (H)
Via Ferruccio 22, 53011
Castellina in Chianti SI. Tel
0577/741186; fax 0577/740386.
(L)(L)
Newly restored hotel in a 14th-
century palace in the centre of
Castellina with comfortable
rooms. The stone-vaulted cellar
houses the *cantina* of the Fattoria
La Castellina, whose wines can
be sampled in the bar.

Ristorante La Toppa (R)
Strada Canaglia 10a, 50020 San
Donato in Poggio FI. Tel
055/8072900. (L)
Good local food as well as some
of the outstanding wines of the
sub-zone.

Antica Trattoria La Torre (R)
Piazza del Comune, 53011
Castellina in Chianti SI. Tel
0577/740236. (L)(L)
Owned and run by the Stiaccini
family for nearly a century, this
fine, classic Tuscan eating house
serves some of the best typical
food of Chianti, including *zuppe
di pane*, meat roasted or grilled
over a wood fire, game and
mushrooms in season.

Bottega del Trenta (R)
Loc. Villa a Sesta, Via Santa
Caterina 2, 53019 Castelnuovo
Berardenga SI. Tel 0577/
359226. (L)(L)
Fresh seasonal produce with a
strong regional accent in this
small, but atmospheric and
highly regarded, winegrower's
favourite. Truffles are the
speciality in season.

Ristorante Vignale (R)
Via XX Settembre 23, 53017
Radda in Chianti SI. Tel 0577/
738094. (L)(L)(L)
Fine, creative cuisine based on
seasonal and local produce marks
this excellent restaurant, long
considered one of the finest in
Chianti. Same ownership as the
nearby Relais Fattoria Vignale
hotel, which has now opened a
more moderately priced *trattoria*.

Ristorante Le Vigne (R)
Podere Le Vigne, 53017 Radda
in Chianti SI. Tel & fax 0577/
738640. (L)(L)

Old house set amid the vineyards
on the edge of Radda in Chianti,
serving mainly locally inspired
dishes at pleasant outdoor tables
in summer.

Albergo Villa Sangiovese
(H)(R)
Piazza Bucciarelli 5, 50020
Panzano FI. Tel 055/852463
(L)(L)(L)
Luxury hotel complex with
comfortable rooms, good
restaurant and swimming pool.
Ideally situated for exploring the
centre of the Chianti Classico
wine zone.

Pecorino *cheese and fresh Tuscan
bread, together with a good bottle of
wine, make an ideal picnic.*

Agriturismo
Badia a Coltibuono
53013 Gaiole in Chianti SI. Tel
0577/749498; fax 0577/749235.
Residential cooking courses with
Lorenza de'Medici on a famous
wine estate.

Podere Capaccia
Loc. Capaccia, 53017 Radda in
Chianti SI. Tel 0574/582426; fax
0574/582428.
Tutored wine-tastings; meals for
groups with Tuscan or medieval
dishes; courses and seminars in
food and wine conducted by
winemaker and food historian
Giampaolo Pacini.

Dievole
53010 Vagliagli SI. Tel 0577/
322613; fax 0577/322574.
Accommodation in bedrooms
and suites in the villa of this
dynamic wine estate. Rented

mainly by the week, although
long weekends (3 nights
minimum) are possible.

Azienda Agricola Pagliarese
53019 Castelnuovo Berardenga
SI. Tel 0577/359070; fax 0577/
359200.
Holiday apartments, wine
tastings, and meals for groups.

Azienda Agricola La Penisola
Loc. La Penisola, 53017 Radda
in Chianti SI. Tel & fax 0577/
738080.
American-owned quiet, peaceful
house in the midst of some of
Radda's most prestigious
vineyards; available for rent
weekly or for weekends out of
season. Swimming pool.

Podere Terreno
Via Terreno alla Via della
Volpaia, 53017 Radda in Chianti
SI. Tel & fax 0577/738312.
Comfortable rooms on a wine
farm. Guests enjoy evening
meals with hosts Sylvie and
Roberto of homecooked local
ingredients and own-produced
Chianti Classico. Served at a
communal table outdoors in
summer or in front of a wood
fire in winter.

expensive

Castello di Uzzano
Via Uzzano 5, 50022 Greve in
Chianti FI. Tel 055/854032; fax
055/854375.
6 beautifully restored, elegantly
furnished apartments in the
courtyard of the villa. Minimum
stay 3 nights.

Castello Vicchiomaggio
Via Vicchiomaggio 4, 50022
Greve in Chianti FI. Tel 055/
854079; fax 055/853911.
Farmhouse apartments in the
Renaissance castle, plus a
restaurant serving fresh, local
produce to residents and to the
public by reservation. Classes on
Tuscan cooking.

Castello di Volpaia
Loc. Volpaia, 53017 Radda in
Chianti SI. Tel 0577/738066; fax
0577/738619.
Magnificent estate located in a
hilltop hamlet, with apartments
to rent by the week.

Wines and Wine Villages

Of all Tuscany's wine zones, Chianti Classico sees the most visitors. Its principal wine towns are Greve, Radda and Castellina, and there are plenty of other smaller, historic towns to visit at the heart of various sub-zones. It is easy enough to get out into the countryside, however, where life takes on a more relaxed pace.

Best producers: *(Chianti Classico)* CASTELL'IN VILLA, *Castello di Bossi, Colle ai Lecci (San Cosma),* FELSINA BERARDENGA, *Le Pici, Poggio Bonelli,* SAN FELICE, *Villa Arceno; (super-Tuscans)* CASTELL'IN VILLA, FELSINA BERARDENGA, *Le Pici, Poggio Bonelli,* SAN FELICE.

Barberino Val d'Elsa Town named after a 14th-century poet, with several fine palaces.

Only part of the commune lies within the Classico zone, but it does include some outstanding individual sites, mostly south-west-facing with a significant percentage of prized *galestro* soils. There is a strong commitment to producing consistently high-quality Chianti Classico (both Normale and Riserva), though there are also very good Sangiovese or Sangiovese-based super-Tuscans. Plantings of Cabernet Sauvignon and Chardonnay remain small.

Best producers: *(Chianti Classico) Casa Emma, Casa Sola, Castello della Paneretta, Le Filigare,* ISOLE E OLENA, MONSANTO, *La Ripa; (super-Tuscans) Casa Emma, La Casetta, Castello della Paneretta, Le Filigare,* ISOLE E OLENA, MONSANTO, *La Ripa, Il Vivaio.*

Castellina in Chianti Small, pretty town, strategically sited on a ridge that runs to the north and south at well over 500m (1650ft) and dominates the surrounding valleys. The front line in the endless wars between Florence and Siena, its walls, fortress and covered walkway provide ample evidence of an embattled past.

The large and diverse commune stretches from just outside Monteriggioni in the south virtually to the centre of the Chianti Classico zone. Many of Castellina's vineyards fan out to the south-west on the spurs that run off the main ridge, the most southern and western reaches becoming progressively more open and gentle. Though there are a number of excellent pockets, the variations in altitude, the jigsaw of soil types and fluctuating climatic conditions from one part to

another mean there may never be any real convergence in style. Cabernet Sauvignon is grown by some producers but it is mostly used in small percentages in Sangiovese-based blends.

Best producers: *(Chianti Classico) Cascina di Cornia,* CASTELLARE DI CASTELLINA, *Castello la Leccia,* CECCHI, FONTERUTOLI, *Lilliano, Nittardi, Rodano,* RUFFINO *(Santedame), San Fabiano Calcinaia, San Leonino;*

The countryside around Castelnuovo Berardenga is open and gently rolling.

(super-Tuscans) Cascina di Cornia, CASTELLARE DI CASTELLINA, CECCHI, FONTERUTOLI, *Lilliano, Rodano.*

Castelnuovo Berardenga This former Sienese stronghold lies just outside the south-eastern corner of the Chianti Classico zone. Here, the countryside is more gently sloping (though rising quite steeply north of San Gusmè) than in Castellina, Radda or Gaiole to the north. Richer, broader wines result from the warmer mesoclimates. There are currently 3 leading producers within the Classico zone – Castell'in Villa, Felsina Berardenga and San Felice – but others are rising rapidly. Cabernet Sauvignon and Chardonnay appear either on their own or in quality blends.

Chianti Classico DOCG The hills between Florence and Siena form Chianti Classico DOCG, an area now expanded from the original Chianti Storico. With over 600 growers and 250 bottlers of wine, it is one of the most important of Italy's wine regions. It was granted its own separate identity in 1995, when some other useful changes in the law were made:

Chianti Classico no longer has to include the white Malvasia or Trebbiano, and may now be made using 100 per cent Sangiovese. The name of an individual registered vineyard may be stated on the label, and Riserva wines can be aged for 2 years instead of 3.

The image of Chianti Classico has now improved considerably among wine consumers. This in turn is giving some producers the confidence to place their often expensive super-Tuscan wine under the Chianti Classico Riserva designation. Prices may, at least initially, prove difficult to maintain, so many of the super-Tuscans names will be kept in order to help maintain the estate's prestige.

There is enormous variation in the quality and style of Chianti Classico. The multiplicity of individual mesoclimates, diverse soils and enormous difference in yields – to say nothing of wine-making competence – make it difficult to ascribe general characteristics at commune level. However, it is generally recognized that Chianti Classico can be some of the best Tuscany has to offer, particularly the Riservas.

For best producers see individual communes:
Barberino Val d'Elsa, Castellina in Chianti, Castelnuovo Berardenga, Gaiole in Chianti, Greve in Chianti, Panzano in Chianti Radda in Chianti, San Casciano Val di Pesa, Tavarnelle Val di Pesa and **Vagliagli.**

Gaiole in Chianti A bustling town in the north of the commune of the same name. It is renowned for its small but often outstanding estates, many with vineyards planted at 400m (1300ft) or more. Good mesoclimates are found throughout, except in the highest eastern ridges in the Chianti hills.

There is a range of wine styles from the austere, elegant, perfumed, long-lived examples of Riecine and Valtellina to broader, fruitier but more accessible ones, such as those of more southerly Rocca di Montegrossi. Refined Chianti from Castello di Ama and San Polo in Rosso highlights the inherent quality of individual vineyards to the west of the commune.

The Sangiovese grape predominates, though there is a little Merlot, Cabernet Sauvignon and Chardonnay, some of it made varietally.
Best producers: *(Chianti Classico)* BADIA A COLTIBUONO, CASTELLO DI AMA, CASTELLO DI BROLIO, CASTELLO DI CACCHIANO, *Montiverdi, Il Palazzino,* RIECINE, *Rietine, Rocca di Castagnoli, Rocca di Montegrossi,* SAN GIUSTO A RENTENNANO, *San Polo in Rosso,* VALTELLINA, *Villa Vistarenni;*

(super-Tuscans) BADIA A COLTIBUONO, *Capannelle,* CASTELLO DI AMA, *Montiverdi, Il Palazzino,* RIECINE, *Rocca di Castagnoli, Rocca di Montegrossi,* SAN GIUSTO A RENTENNANO, *San Polo in Rosso,* VALTELLINA.

Galestro A brand name for wines made from unwanted Malvasia and Trebbiano used previously for Chianti (especially prior to the DOCG upgrade in 1984). While not exciting stuff,

The tiny streets of the medieval village of Panzano are fascinating to wander through.

it was, at least initially, a great commercial success for the large producers who championed it.

More importantly, the name was borrowed from that for a friable marl soil which is found in some of the best vineyards in the Classico zone and elsewhere in Tuscany.

Greve in Chianti One of the major towns of the Classico zone and a bustling market centre. Greve also lends its name to the largest commune of the Classico zone and many of the most successful Cabernet-based or Cabernet-Sangiovese blends can be found here. In the south, around Panzano and Lamole, are some of the finest vineyard sites in Tuscany – as might be expected, Greve has the greatest number of exceptional producers in Chianti Classico. North of the town, however, quality quickly plummets – a large swathe of vineyards at significantly lower altitudes and on heavy clay soils

(excluded from the historic zoning of 1716) really ought to be delisted.
Best producers: *(Chianti Classico)* Carpineto, Casaloste, CASTELLO DI QUERCETO, *Castello di Uzzano,* CASTELLO DI VERRAZZANO, CASTELLO DI VICCHIOMAGGIO, QUERCIABELLA, RUFFINO *(Nozzole, Villa Zano),* Savignola Paolina, VECCHIE TERRE DI MONTEFILI, *Vignamaggio, Viticcio, Villa Cafaggio;* *(super-Tuscans)* Carpineto, CASTELLO DI QUERCETO, CASTELLO DI VERRAZZANO *Poggio Scalette,* QUERCIABELLA, RUFFINO, VECCHIE TERRE DI MONTEFILI, *Vignamaggio, Villa Cafaggio.*
For producers in Panzano *frazione* see **Panzano in Chianti.**

Monti in Chianti In the south of the Gaiole commune; centre for a number of important wine estates and a source of grapes for others. Being further south, and grown in lower altitudes, the wines tend to be concentrated and fuller, though not lacking in finesse. Il Palazzino and San Giusto a Rentennano are particularly outstanding, while Badia a Coltibuono has its vineyards and new winery here.

Panzano in Chianti Beautifully sited village on the end of a ridge, preserving part of its medieval buildings and fortification. Its Romanesque Pieve San Leolino commands a hilltop, and features an imposing 16th-century porch.

The wines of the *frazione,* which is sometimes described as the Conca d'Oro, can be among the most refined, balanced expressions of Chianti Classico. Here, on this arc of south-west facing slopes above the Pesa stream, the heavy clays prevalent in the north of Greve are replaced in part by *galestro,* considered ideal for fine wine.

While the Cabernet Sauvignon grape seems as much at home as the very successful Sangiovese, there have also been some good results with Pinot Nero and Syrah.

Castello dei Rampolla, Fontodi and Villa Cafaggio are

among the Classico leaders, but their ranks have recently been bolstered by the likes of fast-rising La Massa and Monte Bernardi.
Best producers: *(Chianti Classico)* *Le Bocce, Carobbio,* CASTELLO DEI RAMPOLLA, *Cennatoio, Le Cinciole, Le Fonti,* FONTODI, *La Massa, Le Masse di San Leolino, Montagliari,* MONTE BERNARDI, *Vignole, Villa Cafaggio; (super-Tuscans) Le Bocce,* CASTELLO DEI RAMPOLLA, *Cennatoio, Le Fonti,* FONTODI, MONTE BERNARDI, *Villa Cafaggio.*

Radda in Chianti One of the major Chianti Classico wine towns, in the heart of the zone. Its medieval walls and streets afford a wide panorama of the surrounding countryside. The Palazzo del Podestà (Governor's Palace) that is now the town hall, decorated with colourful plaques and coats of arms, is worth a look.

Despite being in the centre of Chianti Classico, there are relatively few top estates in the commune itself. North and north-east of the village are the high slopes of the Monte dei Chianti, whose peaks mark the eastern limit of the zone. Here, situated in a relatively tight cluster (though poorly linked by road) are Radda's finest estates. Soils in the best sites are predominantly prized *galestro* and limestone-rich *alberese.*

Although there are some plantings of Cabernet Sauvignon, Sangiovese either dominates or is used exclusively in the best super-Tuscans.
Best producers: *(Chianti Classico)* CAPACCIA, *Castello d'Albola,* CASTELLO DI VOLPAIA, *Colle Bereto,* MONTEVERTINE, *Petroio (alla via della Malpensata), Podere Terreno, Poggerino, Pruneto, Vignavecchia; (super-Tuscans)* CAPACCIA, CASTELLO DI VOLPAIA, *Colle Bereto,* MONTEVERTINE, *Petroio (alla via della Malpensata), Vignavecchia.*

Sant'Andrea in Percussina
The Consorzio del Marchio Storico Chianti Classico is based in this small village, although it is due to relocate to Radda in Chianti in the year 2000. Also home to the Florentine strategist

Niccolò Macchiavelli while he was writing his famous treatise, *Il Principe (The Prince).*

San Casciano Val di Pesa
The largest town in Chianti Classico – its historic heart is attractive and lively. There are a number of churches and buildings to visit, including the Collegiata, the Chiesa di Santa Maria del Gesù and the late

The buildings of the Castello di Volpaia estate dominate the hamlet of Volpaia.

13th-century Chiesa di San Francesco. Especially notable is Chiesa di Santa Maria del Prato with its beautiful Renaissance religious pieces – one of the richest collections in the zone.

For super-vintners Antinori, this is the centre of wine-making operations for estates located to the south and east. Much of the wine commune, like the northern part of Greve, was only included in Chianti Classico following an extension to the historic boundaries in 1932. But Antinori's Santa Cristina and Pèppoli estates are doing much to raise the commune's profile.
Best producers: *(Chianti Classico)* ANTINORI, CASTELLI DEL GREVEPESA, *Fattoria delle Corti (recent vintages), Massanera; (super-Tuscans)* ANTINORI, *Massanera.*

San Gusmè Picturesque village in the northern part of the commune of Castelnuovo Berardenga. The surrounding *frazione* includes the San Felice, Villa Arceno and Colle ai Lecci estates.

Tavarnelle Val di Pesa Like Barberino Val di Elsa, this town is just outside the western edge of the Classico boundaries. Only about half of this commune falls inside the zone, but the part north of the Pesa stream is essentially a north-western continuation of Panzano's slopes. If not quite so favoured as Panzano, the commune's undoubted potential has been highlighted by Antinori by transforming the wines from the abbey of Badia a Passignano. Although there are only a few good producers within the Classico boundaries, there are other worthy estates in the commune, whose wines are sold as vini da tavola or Chianti dei Colli Fiorentini.
Best producers: *(Chianti Classico)* ANTINORI *(Badia a Passignano), Il Poggiolino, Poggio al Sole; (super-Tuscans)* ANTINORI, *Il Poggiolino.*

Vagliagli This picturesque village is the hub of a *frazione* in the south of the Chianti Classico zone, home to a handful of good or improving estates.
Best producers: *(Chianti Classico)* *Fattoria dell'Aiola, Borgo Scopeto,* DIEVOLE, *Terrabianca; (super-Tuscans) Fattoria dell'Aiola, Terrabianca.*

Volpaia The pretty hamlet of Volpaia was once a Florentine military stronghold. Important now for its leading wine estate, Castello di Volpaia.

Siena

Siena, Florence's great rival, is a mainly late medieval town, its narrow, stone-paved streets, steep alleys and noble palaces little changed in centuries. Sited on three steep hills, Siena is considerably smaller than Florence, and today the former independent republic is mainly a city of art, architecture and tourism. Siena has few good restaurants and accommodation is hard to find in the historic centre. However, the city makes an excellent base for exploring the famous wine country that lies all around it: Chianti Classico, San Gimignano, Montalcino and Montepulciano. While there is no shortage of shops selling wine, there are few good local bars. But Siena's great gastronomic forte is its sweets, most notably *panforte* – don't leave without sampling it.

Siena's fan-shaped central square, the Campo, is the hub of city life, although it offers no gastronomic bargains. For cheaper and more authentic Tuscan bars and restaurants, head out a little from the city centre.

Siena Fact File

Siena is a city for exploring on foot. In any case, you must leave your car outside (the Stadium is a good place to park).

Information

APT
Via di Città 43. Tel 0577/42209.

Ufficio Informazioni Turistiche
Piazza del Campo 56. Tel 0577/ 280551.

Markets

Wednesday morning (street stalls surround the Medici fortress near the Stadium).

Festivals and Events

Siena's *Palio* is probably the most famous festival in Italy. The bareback horse race between riders from each of the town's *contrade* (quarters) takes place on 2 July and 16 August around the Campo.

The *Settimana dei Vini* in the first half of June is a week dedicated to enjoying wine, with various events and initiatives organized by, and often taking place at, the Enoteca Italiana.

Enoteche and Bars

Enoteca Italiana
Fortezza Medicea.
Italy's only national, publicly funded wine showcase, located in the Medici fortress. This is an important point of reference for

all Italian wines. In particular, there are displays representing virtually every DOC and DOCG in Tuscany. Most can be sampled, and all purchased.

Antica Drogheria Manganelli
Via di Città 71/73.
Founded in 1879, this traditional shop is a good source for homemade *dolci senesi*, especially *panforte*, as well as Tuscan wines and *grappe*.

Enoteca I Terzi
Via dei Termini 7.
A recently opened *enoteca*/wine bar near the Campo with an impressive selection of wines available by the glass. The wines (from Tuscany, other areas of Italy and the world) can be sampled in the vaulted tasting area, together with snacks, light meals or a *menù degustazione*, when each course is accompanied by a specially selected wine.

Enoteca San Domenico
Via del Paradiso 56.
Siena's finest wine shop, near the Stadium, offers examples of the best Tuscan wines. Some older vintages are available, plus a good selection of super-Tuscans, *grappe* and *dolci senesi*.

Where to Eat

Antica Trattoria Botteganova Ⓡ
Via Chiantigiana 29. Tel 0577/ 284230; fax 0577/271519.
ⓁⓁⓁ
Located just outside Siena, this *trattoria* serves excellent traditional and creative food. The wine list is extensive and fairly priced.

Il Campo Ⓡ
Piazza del Campo 50. Tel 0577/ 280725. ⓁⓁ
Perhaps the best bet for dining on the Campo. It serves both local and national dishes. In season, dine outdoors.

Le Logge Ⓡ
Via del Porrione 33. Tel 0577/ 48013. ⓁⓁ
Siena's most *simpatico* (if sometimes chaotic) restaurant in an alley near the Campo. Dine at street-side tables under gas lights, or in the dining-room, on mainly seasonal and traditional foods. The house Rosso di Montalcino is made by the owner and is excellent.

La Torre Ⓡ
Via Salicotto 7/9. Tel 0577/ 287548. Ⓛ
This family-run *trattoria* is a reliable place for simple but ample home-cooked meals. The house wine is acceptable.

The rolling, open countryside to the south-west of San Gimignano is as pleasing to the eye as the unique skyline of the *città delle belle torri* itself. An area still not wholly given over to monoculture, olive groves and farm plots create a harmonious patchwork interspersed with the more intensive, specialized cultivation of vines. Though new varieties are being planted within the zone, this is still the kingdom of Vernaccia, Tuscany's most characterful indigenous white grape variety, whose name is probably derived from the Latin *vernaculus* – thus indicating its native provenance. The zone's finest vineyards are planted on slopes with south-western through south-eastern aspects. The open, undulating calcareous sand and sandy loam terrain is well ventilated, an important factor for the health of the mildew-prone Vernaccia.

Wherever you are in the wine zone, the towers of San Gimignano are rarely out of sight – as here, in the autumnal vineyards between the estates of Pietraserena and Pietrafitta.

San Gimignano

Famous for its remarkable medieval skyline, San Gimignano – *la città delle belle torri* (the city of beautiful towers) – is at the centre of a zone also renowned for its characterful white wines, produced from the indigenous Vernaccia grape. Grown on calcareous sands and sandy loams over exposed, gently rolling hills, the best wines, sometimes oak-aged, can develop a nutty complexity.

The Tour

Poggibonsi, the starting point of the tour, is a rather unexciting town on the old Roman Via Cassia. Heading west, the first large winery is Casa alla Terra, the co-operative cellars for over a hundred small growers making a full range of sound, if rarely exhilarating, wines. A little further on, a track to the right passes Pietrafitta, one of the oldest estates in the zone, which claims the region's first Vernaccia plantings in 1280. There is good Chianti and Vin Santo, and the Riserva is the most noteworthy of the various Vernaccias – all available from the *vendita diretta*.

Continue along the track, catching the fine views of San Gimignano. This terrain is typical of the zone: undulating hills that are never too steep, are well-exposed to the sun, with good through breezes – important for preventing diseases such as powdery mildew attacking the grapes. Further along is Pietraserena, source of characterful Vernaccia Vigna del Sole and good Chianti Colli Senesi Poggio al Vento.

The dirt track finally meets the main road, with the Romanesque Pieve di Casale on the left. A sharp right leads to one of San Gimignano's foremost estates, Teruzzi & Puthod's Ponte a Rondolino, whose modern winery, with its stainless steel, temperature-controlled fermentation vats standing outside, lies in a hollow in the hills. The flagship wine is Terre di Tufi, a Vernaccia with a striking designer bottle and postage-stamp-sized label that continues to be one of the most sought-after Tuscan whites.

Back on the paved road, almost immediately to the right is Baroncini – try the Vernaccia di San Gimignano Riservas, notably the Dometaia Cru. Nearby Casale-Falchini, another top estate, demonstrates the potential of the region with up-to-the-minute technology, producing serious Vernaccia and the Cabernet Sauvignon Campora (one of the zone's finest and most famous red wines). The sparkling Vernaccia, made from Pinot Nero and Chardonnay using the classic Champagne method, is one of the best of its kind.

San Gimignano itself is one of the most remarkable small towns in Italy. Climb the 200-odd steps of the Torre Grossa to look out across lovely wine country. To the west is the

TOUR SUMMARY

A pleasant excursion to the town of San Gimignano by way of its wine country, beginning in Poggibonsi and ending in Certaldo, with its interesting medieval quarter.

Distance covered   30km (19 miles).

Time needed   2 hours, not including time for a walking tour of San Gimignano town, for which allow a further 2 hours.

Terrain   The main roads leading to San Gimignano are surfaced and easy to drive. Exploration of the wine country, however, is on rough tracks.

Hotels   There are good hotels in both San Gimignano town centre as well as throughout the wine country.

Restaurants   The best choice of restaurants – local as well as more up-market – is in San Gimignano itself.

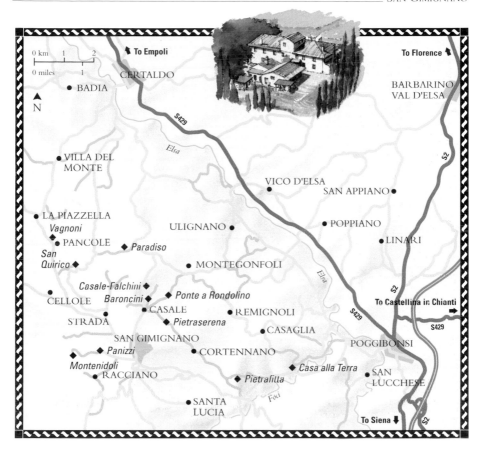

Map of the San Gimignano wine region showing towns and estates including Certaldo, Badia, Villa del Monte, La Piazzella, Vagnoni, Pancole, San Quirico, Paradiso, Cellole, Casale-Falchini, Baroncini, Strada, Ponte a Rondolino, Casale, Pietraserena, San Gimignano, Panizzi, Montenidoli, Racciano, Remignoli, Cortennano, Casaglia, Santa Lucia, Pietrafitta, Casa alla Terra, Ulignano, Montegonfoli, Vico d'Elsa, San Appiano, Poppiano, Linari, Poggibonsi, San Lucchese, Barbarino Val d'Elsa. Routes: To Empoli, To Florence, To Castellina in Chianti, To Siena.

highest vineyard and line of cypress trees that mark Montenidoli and, below, the Panizzi estate; to the north lie some of the zone's best sites, including Vagnoni, San Quirico and Cesani; just visible to the northeast and east are Ponte a Rondolino, Pietraserena and Pietrafitta.

Leave the town by the western Porta San Giovanni, taking the dirt track that leads to Panizzi, whose ageworthy Vernaccia Riserva is one of the zone's best; and Montenidoli, whose range of Vernaccia is fascinating: Fiore, produced from free-run juice, is floral, delicately fruity but with good body; Tradizionale, rather more rustic and robust; and Caratto, vinified and aged in barrique, sleeker, softer, more international in style, but the most ageworthy.

Return through San Gimignano and head north toward Certaldo, stopping at San Quirico, source of well-priced Vernaccia and Riserva. Pancole, a small but atmospheric hamlet about ten minutes' drive further on, is one of the best sectors of San Gimignano. Other key estates in this area include the small family run Vagnoni, whose best wine is an increasingly fine Cru Vernaccia called Mocali, and Paradiso.

Finish the tour in Certaldo, a modern town with an atmospheric medieval upper quarter that is the birthplace of Boccaccio, the lusty author of the *Decameron*.

Map illustration: Teruzzi & Puthod's Ponte a Rondolino estate.

San Gimignano Fact File

Medieval San Gimignano attracts its fair share of visitors. At the busiest time of year, May to October, the town can become very crowded, and accommodation is hard to find – book ahead if possible.

Information
APT
Piazza Duomo 1, 53037 San Gimignano SI. Tel 0577/ 940008; fax 0577/940903.

Consorzio della Denominazione San Gimignano
Villa della Rocca, 53037 San Gimignano SI. Tel 0577/ 940108; fax 0577/942088.

Markets
San Gimignano – Thursday

Festivals and Events
San Gimignano celebrates its *Festa Patronale* (patronal festival) on 31 January, while *Carnevale* (before Lent in mid-February) is another perfect excuse in the wine commune for a major outdoor party.

In mid-June, the town stages the *Cavaliere di Santa Fina* which includes horse races and equestrian exhibitions, and the locals dress up in medieval costumes.

As a designated *città del vino* – city of wine – San Gimignano is the venue for an annual international symposium on wine-related topics.

Enoteche and Bars
Virtually every shop in San Gimignano, no matter what its principal business, offers wine for sale to passing tourists.

The Fattoria Cusona, one of the zone's long-standing producers, has its own outlet for tasting and direct sales in the Piazza San Agostino, to the north of the town.
Enoteca Il Castello
Palazzo Gonfiantini, Via del Castello 20, 53037 San Gimignano SI.
Sample an extensive range of San Gimignano's finest wines in a comfortable and historic setting not far from the main square.

The towers of San Gimignano, spectacular medieval skyscrapers, are remarkably well-preserved.

Enoteca Da Gustavo
Via San Matteo 29, 53037 San Gimignano SI.
Not far from the Duomo, this is the best wine shop in town, an excellent place to sample wines by the glass or bottle, together with simple, well-prepared *spuntini* (snacks).

Enoteca Casa del Caffè
Via San Matteo 2, 53037 San Gimignano SI.
Good wine shop and general store, run by an enthusiastic and knowledgeable wine lover. Also good *salumi di cinghiale* and other general groceries, as well as quality Vernaccias available chilled for a picnic in the vineyards.

Where to Stay and Eat
Ristorante Bel Soggiorno Ⓗ Ⓡ
Via San Giovanni 91, 53037 San Gimignano SI. Tel 0577/ 940375; fax 0577/943149. Ⓛ Ⓛ Ⓛ
The restaurant of this traditional hotel serves refined and creative Tuscan food in the light and spacious dining-room that enjoys splendid panoramic views over the surrounding vineyards and olive groves. Excellent wine list including good selection by the glass.

Osteria delle Catene Ⓡ
Via Mainardi 18, 53037 San Gimignano SI. Tel 0577/ 941966. Ⓛ
Classic Tuscan *trattoria* serving freshly prepared traditional dishes, together with a good selection of Vernaccia and other fine wines from Tuscany. Don't miss the stupendous *anitra col cavolo nero* (duck cooked with winter cabbage).

Hotel La Cisterna Ⓗ Ⓡ
Piazza della Cisterna 23, 53037 San Gimignano SI. Tel 0577/940328; fax 0577/ 942080. Ⓛ Ⓛ
Centrally located traditional hotel on the main square, set in a former 14th-century convent, its 50 rooms furnished with antique Florentine furniture. The fine restaurant, Le Terrazze, serves well-prepared regional food in a terraced dining-room which enjoys magnificent views of the surrounding countryside.

Dorandò Ⓡ
Vicolo dell'Oro 2, 53037 San Gimignano. Tel 0577/941862. Ⓛ Ⓛ Ⓛ
Elegant, well-prepared food: light and innovative *cucina toscana rivisitata* and interesting dishes inspired by medieval and even Etruscan tastes, plus an excellent, fairly priced wine list.

Hotel Leon Bianco Ⓗ
Piazza della Cisterna, 53037 San Gimignano SI. Tel 0577/ 941294; fax 0577/942123. Ⓛ Ⓛ
Located opposite Hotel La Cisterna on San Gimignano's main square, a friendly family hotel in an old historic palace. No restaurant but useful private parking facility.

Trattoria La Mangiatoia Ⓡ
Via Mainardi 5, 53037 San Gimignano SI. Tel 0577/ 941528. Ⓛ
Popular rustic *trattoria* serving well-prepared *cucina casalinga* – *pappardelle ai funghi*, grilled meats, wild boar – and equally rustic Vernaccia wine, produced in its own vineyards.

Hotel Pescille Ⓗ
Loc. Pescille, 53037 San
Gimignano SI. Tel & fax
0577/940186. ⓁⓁ
Well-equipped hotel located
3km (2 miles) south of San
Gimignano on the road to Castel
San Gimignano. Set in a former
fortress and convent, it has
splendid views across to San
Gimignano. There is a
swimming pool but, at present,
no restaurant.

Hotel Le Renaie ⒽⓇ
Loc. Pancole, 53037 San
Gimignano SI. Tel 0577/955044;

fax 0577/955126. ⓁⓁ
Located about 5km (3 miles)
north of San Gimignano in the
hamlet of Pancole. This modern
hotel has spacious, well-equipped
rooms, as well as a swimming
pool and a well-regarded
restaurant, Il Leonetto, which
specializes in local game, wild
mushrooms and truffles in season.
There is also a good wine list.

Agriturismo
**Azienda Agricola
Montenidoli**
Loc. Montenidoli, 53037
San Gimignano SI. Tel

0577/941565; fax 0577/942037.
Apartments for rent in the heart
of the San Gimignano wine
country. The owners also
organize wine-tastings and
seminars for groups.

**Azienda Agrituristica
Monchino**
Loc. Casale 12, 53037 San
Gimignano SI. Tel 0577/
941136; fax 0577/943042.
Eleven well-appointed rooms
situated on a working wine
estate not far from San
Gimignano. Facilities include a
swimming pool.

Wines and Wine Villages
Aside from the busy town of San Gimignano itself, the
zone's villages are quiet and the surrounding countryside
dotted with vineyards and wine estates.

**Chianti dei Colli Senesi
DOCG** One of the 7 Chianti
sub-zones. Wines qualify for the
same AC as that made as far
away as Montepulciano, simply
because the area in which they
are made lies in the province of
Siena. Although they tend to be
light, the wines can show
surprising colour, vigour and
perfume.
Best producers: Baroncini, CASALE-
FALCHINI, *Vincenzo Cesani,*
MONTENIDOLI, PANIZZI, *Pietrafitta,*
PIETRASERENA, *La Rampa di
Fugnano, Vagnoni.*
See also p.71.

Pancole An emerging sub-
zone for some of the best
Vernaccia, centred on the small
hamlet of the same name.

San Gimignano DOC A
new DOC (from the 1997
vintage) that will include red,
rosato and vin santo. This should
incorporate existing red super-
Tuscan as well as the somewhat
misplaced Chianti dei Colli
Senesi, so strengthening the
image of the zone as a whole.

*The vineyards below the hamlet of
Pancole are gaining a reputation for
producing some of the best Vernaccia.*

At its centre, Tuscany's best
surviving medieval town is
famous chiefly for its soaring
skyline of 13 towers, and is
perhaps most remarkable when
viewed from a distance. Among
its many sights, the 11th-century
Collegiata and the Palazzo del
Popolo are well worth a visit.
Within the surrounding
commune, zonal differences are
small, and so changes in wine
character owe more to vineyard
practices and wine-making
expertise. In addition to white
Vernaccia, most estates produce
Chianti dei Colli Senesi.

Many also make superior super-
Tuscan, oak-aged Sangiovese-
based reds.
Best producers: (super-Tuscans)
CASALE-FALCHINI, MONTENIDOLI,
PANIZZI, PIETRASERENA, *La Rampa
di Fugnano, Guicciardini Strozzi,*
TERUZZI & PUTHOD, *Vagnoni.*

**Vernaccia di San Gimignano
DOCG** Dry white wine
which has been DOCG only
since 1993. The best are
increasingly characterful,
especially in Riserva versions.
Best producers: Baroncini, CASALE-
FALCHINI, *Vincenzo Cesani,*
Guicciardini Strozzi,
MONTENIDOLI, PANIZZI, *Paradiso,*
Pietrafitta, PIETRASERENA, *La
Rampa di Fugnano, San Quirico,*
TERUZZI & PUTHOD, *Vagnoni.*

The tiny walled village of Bolgheri is at the centre of a brand new wine zone, Bolgheri Sassicaia DOC, which was created for its most famous wine, Sassicaia.

Bolgheri and the Etruscan Coast

Tuscany's newest great wine zone, Bolgheri, has become internationally famous, thanks to the high profile of its greatest wines, Sassicaia and Ornellaia, but the area from which they originate is quiet in the extreme. Super-Tuscan wines (especially Cabernets) are at their pinnacle here, due in part to a special mesoclimate. As well as an exploration of this tiny but prestigious zone, the tour offers the chance to visit the up-and-coming wine zones of Montescudaio DOC to the north, and Val di Cornia DOC in the south.

The Tour

Volterra, a steep, ancient hill town of Etruscan origin, is the starting point for the tour. From here, strike out into the sparse, empty hills for the small medieval village of Montecatini Val di Cécina, located within the Montescudaio DOC, and home of Sorbaiano, one of its finest producers, noted for fine Cabernet-based Rosso delle Miniere.

From Montecatini, head along the Cécina Valley to Montescudaio, a hill village commanding the plain leading down to the sea. There is a handful of producers around and just outside the town, but two of the best are located a little way out from Montescudaio. Poggio Gagliardo, with its fine Sangiovese-Cabernet blend Rovo and fresh Linaglia white, is down from Montescudaio on the road to Cécina, while Tenuta del Terriccio is to the north of Cécina. This is one of Tuscany's up-and-coming new wave wineries and is well worth seeking out for its richly concentrated flagship wine, the Cabernet-Merlot Lupicaia, as well as the intense Rondinaia, a white from the unusual blend of Chardonnay, Sauvignon and Gewürztraminer.

Now head south to Bolgheri, a charming, tiny walled village with a 16th-century castle that was once part of the feudal estate of the della Gherardesca. In the little tree-lined square is the house where the poet Carducci (1835–1907) lived as a child, and a terracotta statue commemorating Nonna Lucia, the subject of one of his poems. His most famous poem, *Davanti San Guido*, is about the hamlet at the other end of the beautiful cypress-lined Via Bolgherese, which has traditionally housed the workers of the Tenuta San Guido estate, the property that brought fame to Bolgheri. The estate's handsome, not overly ornate yellow-gold villa is about 1.5km (1 mile) down the Via Bolgherese. Its famous wine, Sassicaia, was Italy's first super-Tuscan, created by the late Marchese Mario Incisa della Rocchetta with the help of his cousin, Piero Antinori. The first

TOUR SUMMARY

Starting in Volterra, the tour heads toward the coast via the Montescudaio zone, then continues south through Bolgheri and Castagneto Carducci, the heart of the wine country. The tour ends in Suvereto.

Distance covered 90km (55 miles).

Time needed 7 hours. Suvereto and Montescudaio are both an hour's easy drive from Castagneto Carducci.

Terrain The tour is an easy drive, over gently sloping hills, mainly using well-surfaced roads.

Hotels There are some good hotels in Volterra, while there are scores more at all prices in the nearby coastal resorts; hotels in the wine country are modest yet comfortable.

Restaurants The wine country offers good, rustic cuisine; there are some fine high-class restaurants on the coast.

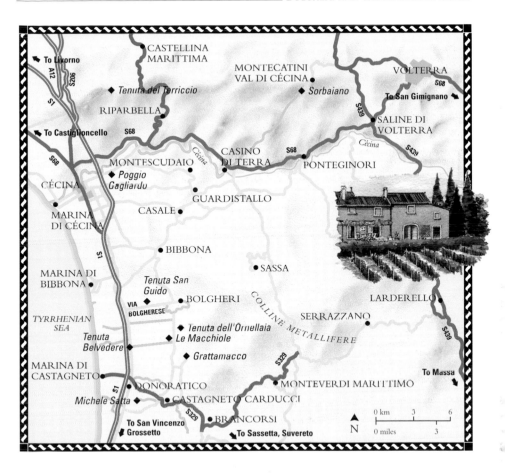

commercial vintage of Sassicaia, vinified in the French manner and aged in new French oak barriques, was 1968, and the wine soon became legendary. Today, the estate is run by Marchese Niccolò Incisa della Rocchetta, who has championed the region and helped to raise its status and prestige; fittingly, from the 1994 vintage, it has become the only individual estate in Italy so far to benefit from its own DOC, Bolgheri Sassicaia.

Continue south from Bolgheri, passing some of the zone's highest-profile vineyards and estates. The Sassicaia vineyard is located on both sides of the road that leads to Castagneto Carducci, an extremely stony, gently sloping site about 100m (300ft) above sea level, planted with 25 year-old Cabernet Sauvignon vines. The road winds round to reveal the imposing gates of Tenuta dell'Ornellaia on the left, the winery set back down a long drive and not visible from the road. When Lodovico Antinori came here in 1981, the lands had been abandoned for nearly a century, so it took considerable effort and immense investment to transform the estate. Today 62ha are planted with vines, and the wines have already achieved great acclaim, notably Ornellaia itself, produced from Cabernet Sauvignon, with Merlot and a

Map illustration: the Grattamacco estate in Castagneto Carducci.

little Cabernet Franc, as well as the rare Masseto, a pure Merlot from a single vineyard that has clay terrain similar to that found in Bordeaux's Pomerol region.

A little further along this stretch is Le Macchiole, source of outstanding, densely concentrated Cabernet-based Paléo Rosso, and fresh, richly textured Paléo Bianco, from Chardonnay, Sauvignon and Vermentino. A detour to the right leads to Tenuta Belvedere, Piero Antinori's Bolgheri estate, whose flagship wine is the Cabernet-Merlot Guado al Tasso — already very good, and likely to compete with Sassicaia and Ornellaia for the zone's top honours.

The estate of Grattamacco is located high up in the hills to the left, and from its commanding position all of Bolgheri's great vineyards are clearly visible: Sassicaia to the right, Ornellaia down below, Guado al Tasso to the left and, just in front, the Santa Teresa estate, where new wines from Angelo Gaja will eventually emerge. Inspired by Sassicaia, Piermario Cavallari began growing Cabernet vines at Grattamacco over 20 years ago, and today his Grattamacco Rosso, produced from Cabernet Sauvignon, Merlot and Sangiovese, is in such demand that from June on, the supply is usually rationed by the single bottle.

At the bottom of the hill just outside Castagneto is the small estate of the young Michele Satta, who uniquely has concentrated on Sangiovese and Vermentino as opposed to French varietals (although he has Syrah and Merlot in production from 1994). Both local grapes find brilliant expression respectively in his top wines, Vigna al Cavaliere and Costa del Giulia.

Castagneto Carducci, a small medieval hill hamlet off the old Via Aurelia between San Vincenzo and Cécina, serves as the centre for the Bolgheri wine zone. The medieval town was sited on the hilltop not just for strategic reasons but also to serve as a refuge from the malaria-ridden lowlands and marshes, parts of which have now been reclaimed. On a clear day, you can see Corsica, as well as the broad arc of the coast extending north toward Cécina, which forms a protective *conca*, or shell, that is responsible in part for the zone's mild, well-ventilated and relatively dry mesoclimate. Castagneto has an excellent *enoteca*, where you can sample and buy rare (and expensive) wines of Bolgheri, and more accessible Montescudaio and Val di Cornia.

Head south for the final part of the tour, winding through the woods to Sassetta and, beyond, to the medieval hill town of Suvereto. This is the centre of the little-known Val di Cornia DOC zone, and, in the surrounding wine hills, a number of remarkably good wines are being produced. Look out for Gualdo del Re, a pure Sangiovese from the estate of the same name, and Giusto di Notri, a Cabernet-Merlot blend from the estate of Tua Rita.

The ground is broken by hand in one of the Cabernet Sauvignon vineyards of Tenuta San Guido, the source of Sassicaia.

Bolgheri Fact File

This still little-visited but exciting wine country is accessible to those staying on the coast or in Volterra.

Information

APT
Piazza Cavour 6, 57100 Livorno.
Tel 0586/898111; fax 0586/896173.

Consorzio di Tutela Vini Bolgheri DOC
Via della Repubblica 15a
57024 Donoratico LI. (No tel.)

Noble Wine Trails
Vietu Viaggi, Piazza Grande 11, 57123 Livorno. Tel 0586/884756; fax 0586/884694. Tailor-made wine tours, with accommodation and winery visits, usually for groups.

Markets

Donoratico – Thursday
Livorno   Mon Sat

Festivals and Events

The biggest local wine and food festival, primarily of interest to professionals, is the *Rassegna Culturale-Enogastronomica Mondovino* in Castagneto Carducci in November.

Enoteche and Bars

The great wines of Bolgheri are always in short supply, and there are few opportunities for tasting and buying at the properties. But wines are available from excellent local *enoteche*.

Enoteca del Borgo
Via V. Emanuele 25/27
57022 Castagneto Carducci LI.
Stylish wine bar/*enoteca* with the wines of Bolgheri by the glass.

Enoteca Maestrini
Via Aurelia 1, Loc. Bambolo
57024 Donoratico LI.
Bolgheri wines, with excellent *salumi, prosciutto* and *pecorino*.

Bar-Alimentari Tognoni
Via Giulia 2, 57022 Bolgheri LI.
Stocks some of the greatest (and most expensive) Italian wines.

Where to Stay and Eat

Nuovo Hotel Bambolo Ⓗ
Loc. Bambolo 31, 57024
Donoratico LI. Tel 0565/775206;
fax 0565/775346. ⓁⓁ
The best hotel in the Bolgheri zone, with spacious modern rooms and a swimming pool.

Enoteca/Ristorante Il Frantoio Ⓡ
Via della Madonna 9, 56040
Montescudaio PI. Tel
0586/650381. Ⓛ
Sample Montescudaio wines with simple local food.

Gambero Rosso Ⓡ
Piazza della Vittoria 1, 57027
San Vincenzo LI. Tel 0565/
701021. ⓁⓁⓁ

Fulvio Pierangelini is one of the great creative chefs of Italy. The menu is constantly changing, and quality is consistently high.

Taverna del Pittore Ⓡ
Largo Nonna Lucia 4, 57022
Bolgheri LI. Tel 0565/762184. Ⓛ
Small, friendly *trattoria*. The well-chosen wine list includes most of Bolgheri's Crus.

Hotel San Lino ⒽⓇ
Via San Lino 26, 56048 Volterra
PI. Tel 0588/85250; fax 0588/
80620. ⓁⓁ
Located in the historic centre, with parking and restaurant.

Ristorante dall'Ugo Ⓡ
Via Pari 3a, 57022 Castagneto
Carducci LI. Tel 0565/763746;
fax 0565/766006. ⓁⓁ
House speciality is pigeon casserole. Extensive wine list.

Hotel-Ristorante Zi' Martino ⒽⓇ
Loc. San Giusto 264a, 57022
Castagneto Carducci LI. Tel
0565/ 766000; fax 0565/
763444. Ⓛ
Rooms with good facilities and a simple family-style restaurant.

Agriturismo

Villa Caprareccia Ⓡ
Via Bolgherese 4, 57020
Bibbona LI. Tel 0586/670128.
Six rooms, camping, swimming pool and an excellent farmhouse restaurant (by reservation).

Wines and Wine Villages

The tiny, medieval wine villages of Bolgheri, Castagneto Carducci and Suvereto are quiet, peaceful places to visit.

Bolgheri DOC Once applied mostly to rosés, but now a rosso superiore category covers all the outstanding new reds. Whites are based on Vermentino, Sauvignon and Trebbiano.
Best producers: (including super-Tuscans) ANTINORI *(Tenuta Belvedere),* GRATTAMACCO, LE MACCHIOLE, *Tenuta dell'Ornellaia,* TENUTA SAN GUIDO *(Sassicaia), Michele Satta.*

Bolgheri Sassicaia DOC
The only single estate in Italy to have its own DOC.

Castagneto Carducci
Medieval hill village above the already fabled wine country.

Montescudaio DOC Large zone, where exciting new wines (including super-Tuscans) are replacing rustic reds and whites.

Best producers: Morazzano, Poggio Gagliardo, SORBAIANO, TENUTA DEL TERRICCIO.

Suvereto Medieval hamlet which is the centre for Val di Cornia wines

Val di Cornia DOC New DOC for Sangiovese-based reds and whites from Trebbiano. Recognition is coming fast.
Best producers: Ambrosini, Jacopo Banti, Gualdo del Re, TUA RITA, *Villa Monte Rico.*

The approach to Montalcino from the north or north-east (Buonvento or Terrenieri) leads through fields of wheat and arable farmland, much dense woodland, and some vineyards. Although it produces some of Italy's most prestigious wines, only eight per cent of the Montalcino commune is planted with vines, while some three-quarters still remains covered by trees and olive groves. Only in the south-western corner of the Montalcino zone, where Banfi has literally changed the face of the terrain, does specialized viticulture predominate. Important sub-zones lie all around the wine town of Montalcino, here visible in its commanding, strategic position on top of the ridge. The northern sub-zone that is illustrated extends across predominantly clay terrain, although the finest sites are located on outcrops of *galestro*, such as the outstanding Cru Montosoli. The buildings to the right in the middle distance are the modern winery of Val di Suga.

The Montosoli hill is the site of some of Montalcino's best vineyards, including that of the Altesino estate, shown here.

Montalcino

Montalcino, an austere, fortified hill town 32km (20 miles) south of Siena, is the centre of one of Italy's premier red wine zones, home of the legendary Brunello di Montalcino DOCG, as well as lighter, less expensive Rosso di Montalcino wines, new wave super-Tuscan whites and reds and Sant'Antimo DOC wines from international and native grapes.

The wine country rises from the undulating *crete senesi,* the eroded clay fields that lie between Montalcino, Siena and Montepulciano, up to a beautiful high ridge of hills bounded by the valleys of the Ombrone to the north and west, and the Asso and Orcia to the east and south. In spite of the fame – and high prices – of its wines, the area remains quiet and peaceful, making an excellent base for walks in unspoiled country, tours of towns such as Pienza and Siena, and exploration of the beautiful Val d'Orcia leading up to Monte Amiata.

The Tour

As the most common approach to Montalcino is from Siena to the north, the tour begins at Buonconvento, a farming community still clustered mainly within its brick, 14th-century town walls along the old Roman Via Cassia. From Buonconvento, head south a couple of kilometres out of town, then look for the provincial road to the right that leads to Montalcino. The town itself is now clearly visible up ahead, dominating the surrounding valleys from its strategic hilltop position. As the land rises, wheatfields soon give way to vineyards. Look for the sign to the left marking an unpaved road that leads to two dynamic, modern estates, Altesino and Caparzo.

Altesino, just beyond the rather dilapidated Castello Altesi, is one of the zone's most welcoming estates, offering tastings and guided tours of the winery. The vanguard of the exciting new investment and thinking of the 1970s and 80s, today Altesino is noted for its modern, powerful Brunellos, especially the outstanding single-vineyard Cru Montosoli, as well as for super-Tuscan wines such as Palazzo Altesi, a sleek Sangiovese aged in barrique.

The dirt road carries on through well-tended vineyards to the neighbouring estate of Caparzo. Its Vigna La Casa Cru, also from the Montosoli hill, is considered one of the finest expressions of Brunello, while the estate has also demonstrated the zone's potential for high-quality white wines in Le Grance, a barrique-fermented Chardonnay.

The tour continues round toward Montalcino. A track to the left leads to the Casanova di Neri farm, a small, well-

TOUR SUMMARY

Starting in Buonconvento, the tour leads through vineyards and wine estates on the approach to the fascinating medieval town of Montalcino, then continues into the principal sub-zones. There are several detours to other important wine estates, before finishing in Montalcino.

Distance covered   50km (30 miles).

Time needed   4 hours.

Terrain   The tour uses a mixture of good surfaced main roads, unpaved roads and poorly surfaced tracks.

Hotels   There are moderate but comfortable hotels in and around the town of Montalcino itself, as well as comfortable *agriturismo* in the outlying countryside.

Restaurants   With one exception in I Poggi, the region's many restaurants are all reasonably priced; they mainly serve hearty local food.

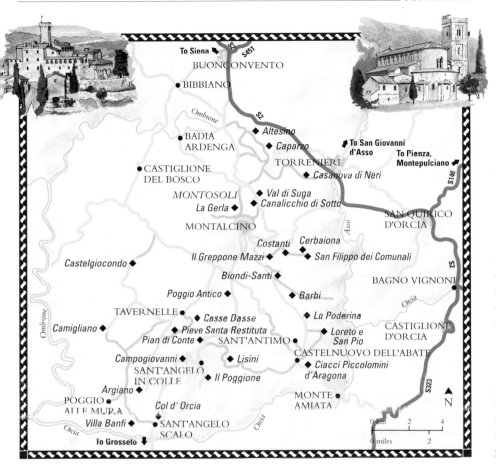

To Siena ↖ S2
S451
BUONCONVENTO
● BIBBIANO
Ombrone
S2
● BADIA
ARDENGA
◆ Altesino
◆ Caparzo
**↗ To San Giovanni
d'Asso**
TORRENIERI
● CASTIGLIONE
DEL BOSCO
◆ Casanova di Neri
**To Pienza,
Montepulciano ➤**
S146
MONTOSOLI
◆ Val di Suga
◆ Canalicchio di Sotto
La Gerla ◆
SAN QUIRICO
D'ORCIA
Asso
MONTALCINO
Costanti   Cerbaiona
Il Greppone Mazzi ◆ ◆   ◆ San Filippo dei Comunali
Biondi-Santi ◆
BAGNO VIGNONI
S2
Castelgiocondo ◆
Poggio Antico ◆
◆ Barbi
Orcia
Ombrone
TAVERNELLE ●
◆ Casse Dasse
◆ La Poderina
CASTIGLIONE
D'ORCIA
Camigliano ◆
◆ Pieve Santa Restituta
Pian di Conte ◆   SANT'ANTIMO ●
◆ Loreto e
San Pio
Campogiovanni ◆
◆ Lisini
CASTELNUOVO DELL'ABATE
◆ Ciacci Piccolomini
d'Aragona
SANT'ANGELO
IN COLLE
◆ Il Poggione
Argiano ◆
MONTE ●
AMIATA
S323
POGGIO ●
ALLE MURA
Col d' Orcia
Orcia
Villa Banfi ◆
● SANT'ANGELO
SCALO
To Grosseto ➤
Orcia
0 km   2   4
0 miles   2
▲ N

run family estate whose best wine is the intensely flavoured Cerretalto Brunello Riserva. The main route, meanwhile, carves through woods and vineyards until it rejoins the paved provincial road just north of the Val di Suga winery which produces vibrant, modern wines. Turning left toward Montalcino, other notable wine estates include the small but superb Canalicchio di Sotto of Maurizio Lambardi, as well as La Gerla. The finest wines from this northern sub-zone are rich, ripe and concentrated, planted at lower altitudes of about 300m (1000ft) on clay with outcrops of limestone (most notably on the slopes of Montosoli and Canalicchio).

The road climbs now to Montalcino itself, and joins another provincial road that connects Torrenieri with Montalcino. Turn left, then find a dirt track to the right that leads to the foremost estate in this eastern sub-zone, Colle al Matrichese, usually known simply as Costanti. The Costantis are an ancient Sienese family whose roots in these parts date back to the 1400s, and who have probably been making wine here since that time from grapes grown on steep, high vineyards surrounding the beautiful family villa. Indeed, the estate's historic Vermiglio del Colle wines

Map illustrations: (above left) the Banfi estate; (above right) the Abbey of Sant'Antimo.

enjoyed fame long before its intense, well-structured and elegant Brunellos. The small production is highly sought after – the Brunello and Riserva are sold on allocation. Other quality estates located on this eastern flank include the tiny but outstanding Cerbaiona, the San Filippo dei Comunali estate, and the Il Greppone Mazzi farm which is managed by the Folonari family of Ruffino fame.

Climb now to Montalcino itself, one of the great wine towns of Tuscany. A small, still mainly intact fortified hill town dominated by its 14th-century Fortezza La Rocca, it is not hard to visualize this stronghold as the final bastion of the Sienese Republic, whose citizens retreated here after Siena itself fell to the Medicis, managing to hold out for another four years. There is a fine *enoteca* within the Fortezza's walls, and scores of other good opportunities to taste and purchase wines.

After visiting Montalcino, continue south, back into the wine country on the road that leads to Castelnuovo dell'Abate and the Abbey of Sant'Antimo. The vineyards that lie along this ridge, joining up with those of Costanti's Colle al Matrichese over the hill, are among Montalcino's highest, the terrain made up of limestone-rich *albarese* and *galestro*. The wines have a reputation for being powerful and structured, with the greatest capacity for aging.

Two historic wine estates lie along this ridge. First is Biondi-Santi, where Brunello di Montalcino was supposedly created over 100 years ago, when Ferrucio Biondi-Santi successfully marketed the wine called Brunello, using a superior clone of the Sangiovese grape. Employing a long fermentation with extended contact between the wines and the skins, the Biondi-Santi family created the blockbuster wines that were to gain world renown for their capacity to age for up to half a century in some cases – and for their incredibly high prices.

The hilltop town of Montalcino is ringed by a fortified wall, and seems little changed since the 16th century.

The Barbi estate, off to the left further toward Sant'Antimo, has long been one of the most dynamic and energetic ambassadors of Montalcino. A traditional, virtually self-contained agricultural estate, it produces not only Brunello and Rosso, but also *salumi* and *pecorino* cheeses from its own herds, all of which can be sampled in its popular *taverna*. The cellars themselves are open for visits, tasting and direct sales without appointment.

From Barbi, continue south, passing La Poderina, an improving estate owned by Saiagricola, an insurance company with extensive agricultural holdings that include Del Cerro in nearby Montepulciano. Standing alone at the head of a valley, surrounded by woodland and vine- and olive-tree-covered hills, the 12th-century Abbey of Sant'Antimo is a fine example of the Romanesque Cistercian style and makes a beautiful spot for a picnic.

The Loreto e San Pio estate of the Mastrojanni family is located on the road to the left, which also leads to Castelnuovo dell'Abate, and comprises a cluster of mainly 13th-century buildings which once housed Santa Caterina of Siena while she was on pilgrimage. The expressive, full-bodied and concentrated wines of Mastrojanni are particularly impressive in the latest releases.

Castelnuovo dell'Abate itself is a small, medieval hamlet that once prospered from its position above Sant'Antimo due to the pilgrim traffic through the Val d'Orcia, and it still retains some monuments from that period. One of these is the medieval Palazzo Patrizio, which remains the seat of the important agricultural estate of Ciacci Piccolomini d'Aragona surrounding Castelnuovo, and is the source of some of the most exciting wines of this area.

From Castelnuovo, find a dirt track leading through woodlands and vineyards across the hills to Sant'Angelo in Colle. About half-way along is the Lisini estate, where consultant Franco Bernabei guides the vinification of first-rate Brunello and Rosso. Bear left at the junction with the paved road and on the right, just before the village, is Pian di Conte, the small estate of the talented Pierluigi Talenti. Once the winemaker at Il Poggione, an extensive traditional estate south of Sant'Angelo, Talenti has been demonstrating here how finely crafted Brunello and Rosso di Montalcino wines of great character and individuality can also be made on a small, artisan scale.

Mixed agriculture – here, vineyards interspersed with olive groves – is a feature of the south-west of the zone.

Head into Sant'Angelo, an atmospheric hill hamlet still almost wholly contained within its circular walls, which affords splendid views across the Orcia Valley toward Monte Amiata, and over the south-western corner of the Montalcino wine zone, scene of the most extensive vineyard planting in recent years. The terrain here is predominantly stony clay, and is more influenced by warm sea breezes, although fog is not uncommon in the pockets beneath the hills. The resulting wines are rich, fleshy and more immediately appealing than the austere styles characteristic of wines from higher vineyards. The Bar-Trattoria Il Pozzo is a good option for some lunch.

Continue south toward Sant'Angelo Scalo, passing the Campogiovanni estate of Chianti Classico producer San Felice – the Brunello can be very good. Further along, next to the remains of a 12th-century castle high on a hilltop, is the 15th-century Villa di Argiano, whose vaulted stone cellars have been beautifully restored. Recently revitalized with help from super-enologist Giacomo Tachis, Argiano's new-style Brunello is generous, fleshy and increasingly concentrated with successive vintages.

Sant'Angelo Scalo, in contrast to its hilltop counterpart, is a dull, modern village on the plain, home to both Villa

Banfi and Col d'Orcia, a large winery owned by the Cinzano group, whose diverse range of wines, including Cabernet, Chardonnay and sweet, grapy Moscadello di Montalcino, is widely distributed both nationally and internationally.

American-owned Banfi is a huge estate of over 800ha of vineyards that dominates the entire southwestern corner of the zone. So seriously does it take its viticulture that in some areas it has reshaped the contours of the land by bull-dozing entire hillsides. Its state-of-the-art winery produces not just premium Brunello and Rosso di Montalcino, but a range of white and red wines from local and international grape varieties. One grape that Banfi revived is Moscadello, used to make a light, sweet sparkling wine, and a luscious, *passito* dessert wine, called simply 'B'.

Follow signs through the intensively planted and well-tended vineyards to the Banfi visitors' centre at Poggio alle Mura, based in the 13th-century Castello Banfi. There is an excellent wine and glassware museum here, as well as a shop stocking the full range of wines.

From Poggio alle Mura, head back toward Montalcino, passing through the sea of Banfi's vineyards – viticulture on a, well, most un-Italian scale. On the right, leading up to Tavernelle, is the Pieve di San Sigisimondo, now an *agriturismo* complex. This is a good place to stop for a bite to eat, or just to have a drink in the *enoteca*, if your throat is parched from the dust of the unpaved roads.

Other quality estates located in the western part of the wine zone can be reached in a detour to the left before Tavernelle. These include the large Camigliano estate, whose winery is centred in a small, once fortified hamlet and palace, as well as Frescobaldi's beautifully restored Castelgiocondo estate. The main route continues through Tavernelle, shortly after which an unpaved track on the right leads to the highly acclaimed Case Basse estate, owned by Milanese stockbroker Gianfranco Soldera, who produces consistently outstanding Brunello wines at Villa Santa Restituta. A near neighbour is Pieve Santa Restituta, centred around an historic Romanesque church that was cited in documents dating from the 8th century. Its Brunello is already fine and Vin Santo outstanding, but since this is where Angelo Gaja has taken an interest, exciting developments are anticipated.

The tour now carries on back to Montalcino: when the road joins the provincial Montalcino-Grosseto road, either return left to Montalcino directly, or else turn right for one final but worthwhile detour, to visit the estate of Poggio Antico, source of very good, if not top-flight, wines, and equally noteworthy for its outstanding restaurant, serving probably the best creative cuisine in the region.

Banfi's vineyards – proudly indicated here by its coat of arms – are spread over a vast area to the south-west of Montalcino.

Montalcino Fact File

There are few hotels in the quiet town of Montalcino, so they can be in heavy demand. However, there are good choices for *agriturismo* and plenty of places to eat and drink.

Information

Pro Loco
Costa del Municipio 8,
53024 Montalcino SI.
Tel 0577/849331.

Consorzio del Vino Brunello di Montalcino
Costa del Municipio 1, 53024
Montalcino SI. Tel 0577/
848246; fax 0577/849425.

Markets

Montalcino – Friday

Festivals and Events

Montalcino celebrates numerous gastronomic festivals, including the *Torneo di apertura delle caccie* on the second Sunday in August to celebrate the start of the hunting season, and the *Settimana del miele*, or honey week, at the start of September. The *Sagra del tordo*, or Festival of the Thrush, on the last Sunday in October, is an opportunity to enjoy autumnal treats such as chestnuts and mushrooms.

San Giovanni d'Asso, famous for its *tartufi bianchi*, or white truffles, has a *Mostra Mercato del Tartufo*, or truffle market, on the third Sunday of November.

Each September the Fattoria dei Barbi organizes the *Premio Internazionale Barbi Colombini*, an important international series of awards for literature and wine journalism.

Enoteche and Bars

More and more *enoteche* open every year in Montalcino. Most are serious wine shops run by devotees, but prices can vary considerably, especially for older vintages – shop around.

Enoteca Bacchus
Via G Matteotti 15, 53024
Montalcino SI.
One of the best places to enjoy a glass of Brunello from the small but good selection, with a wooden platter of cold meats or cheeses. Outdoor tables.

Biondi Santi's wines, here displayed at its tasting room, fell from favour, but are now making a comeback.

Enoteca Collina d'Italia
Via Traversa dei Monti 214,
53024 Montalcino SI.
Located on the sharp bend of the road leading up to Montalcino, this wine shop is owned by Altesino, but stocks wines from other leading producers, too. Wines can be sampled in the adjoining *osteria* (see below).

Enoteca La Fortezza
Piazzale Fortezza, 53024
Montalcino SI.
Located in the 13th-century Rocca, or fortress). Almost all estate bottlings are represented, and a range of wines is always available for tasting. Snacks and outdoor tables in the courtyard.

Enoteca Drogheria Franci
Piazzale Fortezza 5, 53024
Montalcino SI.
A good selection of Brunello and super-Tuscans, especially from the best older vintages. Also superlative honey.

Caffè Fiaschetteria Italiana
Piazza del Popolo 6, 53024
Montalcino SI.
The town's most stylish bar, serving a good range of Brunello and Rosso di Montalcino. The adjoining *cantina* has a good selection of wines for purchase.

Where to Stay and Eat

Taverna dei Barbi Ⓡ
Fattoria dei Barbi, 53024
Montalcino SI. Tel 0577/
848277. ⒧Ⓛ
Long-standing and popular farmhouse restaurant on the Barbi wine estate, serving produce from the farm (excellent *salumi* and *pecorino*) and food served in stylish rustic surroundings. There are cellar visits and direct sales of wines and other products of the estate.

Antica Osteria del Bassomondo Ⓡ
53020 Castelnuovo dell'Abate SI. Tel 0577/835619. Ⓛ
Country *osteria* situated near the abbey of Sant'Antimo, serving well-prepared local food, accompanied by Vasco Sassetti Rosso and Brunello di Montalcino wines. The bar will make *panini* for a picnic.

Hotel-Ristorante al Brunello di Montalcino Ⓗ Ⓡ
Loc. Bellaria, 53024 Montalcino SI. Tel 0577/849304; fax 0577/
849430. ⓁⓁ
A modern, friendly hotel just outside Montalcino on the road to Sant'Angelo and Grosseto. The individually furnished rooms are comfortable and well-equipped, and there is a good restaurant that specializes in game. The fine wine list has Brunellos from every producer in the zone. Swimming pool.

Hotel dei Capitani Ⓗ
Via Lapini 6, 53024 Montalcino SI. Tel & fax 0577/847227.
ⓁⓁ
A 17th-century building newly converted into a 3-star hotel with 29 rooms and 4 suites. Ask for a room at the rear to enjoy magnificent views to the north across the wine country and, beyond, the *crete senesi*. Small swimming pool. Parking.

L'Osteria Collina d'Italia Ⓡ
Via Traversa dei Monti 214,
53024 Montalcino SI. Tel 0577/
847134. Ⓛ
Informal roadside *osteria* serving

one-course and full meals (there is a cold buffet in summer).

Albergo Il Giglio (H)
Via S Saloni 5, 53024
Montalcino SI. Tel & fax 0577/
848167. (D)(L)
Comfortable, newly refurbished
3-star hotel situated conveniently
in the town centre.

Antica Trattoria Il Moro (R)
Via Mazzini 44, 53024
Montalcino SI. Tel 0577/
849384. (L)
Friendly family-style *trattoria*.
The place the locals come to for
pinci, rabbit stewed in Brunello,
and grilled meats. Small but
good wine list.

Ristorante Poggio Antico (R)
Az. Ag. Poggio Antico, Loc. I
Poggi, 53024 Montalcino SI. Tel
& fax 0577/849200. (D)(L)(L)
The finest and most elegant
restaurant in the zone. Refined
cuisine based on fine local
ingredients, presented and served
with style. The wine list is
international, with some pricy
top French offerings (the only
Brunello is the estate wine).

**L'Osteria di Porta al
Cassero** (R)
Via Ricasoli 32, 53024
Montalcino SI. Tel 0577/
847196. (L)

One of Montalcino's best
options for authentic traditional
food – *crostini ai funghi, minestra
di pane, scottiglia* – prepared with
care. There is an excellent
selection of wines. Always
packed, so try to book ahead
if possible.

Bar-Trattoria Il Pozzo (R)
Piazza del Pozzo 2, 53020
Sant'Angelo in Colle SI. Tel
0577/864015. (L)
Local bar-*trattoria* in the centre of
the medieval *borgo* serving *cucina
casalinga: zuppa di pane*,
homemade pasta, *scottiglia, coniglio
ripieno*, and a good selection of
Brunello and Rosso di
Montalcino.

*Montalcino's enoteche are plentiful,
although prices of wines can often
vary between them.*

Agriturismo
Fattoria del Colle
53020 Trequanda SI. Tel 0577/
662108; fax: 0577/849356.
Rustic but comfortable
apartments on a wine and olive
oil estate between Montalcino
and Montepulciano. They can
be rented for 3 days or by the
week. Swimming pools, tennis.

La Crociona
Via Pantaneto 88, Loc. La
Croce, 53024 Montalcino SI.
Tel & fax 0577/848007.
Comfortable mini-apartments by
the night or week in this small
borgo between the Barbi and
Biondi-Santi estates. Pool.

Fattoria Pieve a Salti (H)(R)
Loc. Pieve a Salti, 53022
Buonconvento SI. Tel & fax
0577/807244.
Large hotel and apartment
complex on working agricultural
estate. The farmhouse restaurant
(open to the public) serves
traditional food using primarily
its own produce.

Pieve di San Sigismondo (R)
Pod. La Pieve 19, Loc. Poggio
alle Mura, 53024 Montalcino SI.
Tel 0577/866026.
Newly converted apartments
near Castello Banfi, together
with a well-regarded restaurant
and *enoteca*.

Wines and Wine Villages

The imposing setting and medieval majesty of the hilltop
town of Montalcino suggest a much longer tradition of
prestige than that recently won by its wines.

**Brunello di Montalcino
DOCG** The first, and for a
long time the only, officially
sanctioned 100 per cent
Sangiovese wine in Tuscany.
The name Brunello, successfully
marketed by Biondi-Santi,
rightly denotes an individual
style of wine, but any reference
to it as a name for a clone of
Sangiovese is misleading.
    The wine is no longer always
the powerful, tannic brute it
once was, needing at least 10
years to soften. The use of new

oak by some, changes in
vinification techniques and a
reduction in time spent in the
barrel mean a number of wines
are now approachable soon after
their release (nearly 5 years from
the vintage date).
    Riserva is a superior selection
that requires 5 years' total aging.
A single vineyard, or Cru, name
increasingly is seen on labels,
with or without Riserva, and
usually implies something better
than Brunello Normale. None of
the wine is cheap.

Best producers: ALTESINO,
ARGIANO, BANFI, BARBI, BIONDI-
SANTI, *La Campana*,
Campogiovanni, CANALICCHIO DI
SOTTO, *Capanna*, CAPARZO,
CASANOVA DI NERI, CASE BASSE,
Castelgiocondo, *La Cerbaiola*,
CERBAIONA, CIACCI PICCOLOMINI
D'ARAGONA, COL D'ORCIA,
COSTANTI, *Due Portine Gorelli*,
Friggiali, Fuligni, La Gerla, Lisini,
MASTROJANNI, SILVIO NARDI, *Siro
Pacenti*, PIEVE SANTA RESTITUTA,
La Poderina, POGGIO ANTICO, *Ol
Poggiole*, IL POGGIONE, TALENTI,
VAL DI SUGA, *Valdicava*.

Castelnuovo dell' Abate
Hamlet just south of the
beautiful abbey of Sant'Antimo.

There are good soils in favourable sites and two of Montalcino's most outstanding producers – Ciacci Piccolomini d'Aragona and Mastrojanni.

Castiglione del Bosco There are few estates or vineyards in this north-western corner of the zone. Significantly Silvio Nardi produces only Rosso from vineyards here – its Brunello comes instead from vines grown on *galestro* soils in the south-east.

Montalcino Medieval town with evidence of Roman, Etruscan and older settlements. The Fortezza provides panoramic views from its 16th-century walls.

The zone is ringed by waterways, its hills rising from an undulating plain of clay. The climate is generally hot, dry and relatively even from year to year. The area can be split into 4 sub-zones, yet the combination of varying soils, altitude, aspect and mesoclimate produce distinct terroirs within each.

In the central-eastern area the Greppi zone produces the classic style of Brunello made famous by Biondi-Santi. The vineyards are often at 400–500m (1300–1650ft) on soils which have some of the clay of the lower lying areas as well as *galestro* and *alberese*. There is none of the maritime influence of the south or south-west. The wines are austere and forbidding when young, but reveal an intense fruit depth and unmistakable class with considerable age. Even the Rosso di Montalcino from Costanti, which epitomizes this style, can require a further 5 years' keeping after release.

Immediately to the north of Montalcino town is an area of relatively intense cultivation. Clay soils predominate but there are good outcrops of *galestro* in vineyards such as Montosoli, adding the finesse that can otherwise be missing.

Vineyards in the western part of the zone are relatively few, but include Frescobaldi's substantial estate of Castelgiocondo. There are

outcrops of *galestro* and *alberese* soil at 300–400m (1000–1300ft).

Virtually everything in the south-western corner belongs to Banfi. The southern area benefits from the Orcia Valley and the maritime influence which it channels up from the coast. But while it is drier and warmer than the other parts of the zone, there is considerable variation within it. The southern-most vineyards are at low altitudes on stony clay. The soils on higher slopes to the north can contain *galestro* and *alberese*.

See also **Castelnuovo dell'Abate**, **Poggio alle Mura**, **Sant'Angelo in Colle** and **Sant'Angelo Scalo**.

Montalcino, with its steep, narrow streets, is essentially a medieval country town.

Moscadello di Montalcino DOC Sweet, grapy dessert wine. There are few modern examples, although the region's reputation for wine in the Middle Ages is thought to have been for something similar.
Best producers: BANFI, COL D'ORCIA.

Poggio alle Mura This, and practically everything else in the south-west corner of the zone, belongs to Banfi.

Sant'Antimo DOC Montalcino is a forward-looking wine region that continues to stay a step ahead. Its most recent initiative is a new DOC for wines from international varieties, such as Cabernet Sauvignon and Chardonnay. At

least some of the super-Tuscans should now become officially sanctioned.

Rosso di Montalcino DOC A younger fruitier style than Brunello, often ready on release (2–3 years from the vintage). The grapes normally come from vines that are younger or less suitable for Brunello, while the amount produced varies considerably from year to year – proportionally more is made in a poorer vintage. While the growth and success of Rosso has done much to maintain the quality of Brunello, in some instances the more modern handling can actually result in a wine of almost comparable stature, yet it sells for around half the price.
Best producers: ALTESINO, ARGIANO, BANFI, BARBI, *La Campana*, CANALICCHIO DI SOTTO, *Capanna*, *Caparzo*, CASANOVA DI NERI, *Castelgiocondo*, *La Cerbaiola*, CIACCI PICCOLOMINI D'ARAGONA, COL D'ORCIA, COSTANTI, *Due Portine Gorelli*, *Friggiali*, *Fuligni*, *La Gerla*, *Lisini*, SILVIO NARDI, *Siro Pacenti*, POGGIO ANTICO, IL POGGIONE, TALENTI, VAL DI SUGA, *Valdicava*.

Sant'Angelo in Colle Quiet, well-preserved medieval hamlet with good views to the south over the Orcia Valley.

The surrounding *frazione* has a number of excellent producers. As the hills rise to the north, marked differences appear in the wines – altitude and aspect change, but there are significant outcrops of *galestro* and *alberese* soils. The dry but moderating influence of the Maremma also plays a part. The wines, with low to moderate acidities, are broader, more powerful but also more accessible than those in the eastern zone.

Sant'Angelo Scalo Dull village at the central-southern entrypoint to the Montalcino zone. Clay predominates and the vineyards are relatively low-lying. The wines can be full and accessible, but they also tend to lack class.

The wine zone of Montepulciano extends down from the eponymous hill town, sited on a ridge of volcanic tufa, across gentle slopes to the wide, flat Chiana Valley, before rising north again to the hills around the town of Valiano. This vineyard is Bindella's Tenuta Vallocaia, planted on a low, well-exposed spur typical of the Montepulciano countryside at around 300m (1000ft). The rows are widely spaced to allow the easy passage of tractors, while the vines within each row have been planted relatively close together, so maintaining a reasonable density. Roses planted at the ends of the rows not only make the landscape more attractive, but also serve a purpose: common vine diseases often attack the rose first, thus allowing preventive treatment to be taken on the vines.

Montepulciano is one of Tuscany's most charming hilltop towns, although the wine country which surrounds it is the real draw for the wine lover.

Montepulciano

Montepulciano, the highest of Tuscany's hilltop towns, rises sharply out of broad vine-covered slopes extending down to the Chiana Valley. Much contested in the historic rivalry between Siena and Florence, its former prosperity is displayed in the palaces and churches that line its principal avenues. Still a working wine centre, with cellars beneath its stone-paved streets which date back to Etruscan times, it is also the hub of a zone whose wines have been enjoyed and praised since the 8th century.

On the steep and narrow spur that dominates the valley one wine reigns supreme – Vino Nobile di Montepulciano, one of Italy's first DOCGs. The so-called noble wine may not have warranted its status initially, but such official recognition served as a spur to local winegrowers and outside investors, who are now making wines of real character and quality. At its best, Vino Nobile is a concentrated yet refined, ageworthy red, but the region also produces notable super-Tuscans, Vin Santo and Rosso di Montepulciano, a lighter, everyday red.

The Town

Montepulciano's strategic position meant that it was long fought over, at no time more fiercely than in the continuing rivalry between Siena and Florence. Florence eventually prevailed and, in 1511, the Marzocco, the regal lion on the tall column by the Porta del Prato, was put up to replace the nursing she-wolf of Siena. The town has considerable charm and style. Its principal avenue, the Corso, extends the length of the town for a over a kilometre, and is lined with stately, mainly Renaissance, palaces as it meanders up to the Piazza Grande. Underneath, the town is riddled with cool caves, hand-carved out of soft rock, some of which date back to Etruscan times. At one time, most of the cellars of the town's palaces were working wineries, although now only a handful of producers continue to vinify and age their wines here. The beautiful Renaissance Tempio di San Biagio, just below the town walls, should not be missed, and there is a fine restaurant, La Grotta, opposite the church.

The zone's most famous wine producer, Avignonesi, has now transferred its wine-making operations to its estates in the outlying countryside, but its adminstration is still carried out in the handsome 16th-century Palazzo Avignonesi, at the bottom end of the Corso. The wine shop in the palace offers the full range of Avignonesi wines – fine Vino Nobile di Montepulciano, Vin Santo, and a range of sleek wines from Cabernet Sauvignon, Merlot, Sauvignon and Chardonnay – and tasting is usually available. Ask to visit

TOUR SUMMARY

A fascinating walking tour of historic Montepulciano and its cellars, followed by an easy circular drive through the wine country, finishing in Pienza.

Distance covered   75km (45 miles).

Time needed   4 hours.

Terrain   The tour through the wine country extends across both surfaced and unpaved roads. The zone is not very well sign-posted, and the roads can sometimes be difficult to follow.

Hotels   There are good, comfortable hotels in the town of Montepulciano, and outstanding options in Montefollonico and Sinalunga; pleasant *agriturismo* in the wine country.

Restaurants   The wine country offers limited choices, although there are some good local restaurants in the town of Montepulciano itself, as well as the luxury restaurants in Montefollonico and Sinalunga.

the 12th-century cellars and Etruscan tomb over which the palace is built.

The most impressive wine cellars in Montepulciano are those of the Cantina del Redi, just off the Piazza Grande. Like a vast, subterranean Renaissance cathedral, its high, vaulted cellars are eerily beautiful, lined with ancient, immense oak and chestnut *botte*. Though no longer a working winery, there is a hand-dug grotto in the deepest part of the cellar that is used to store the finest Reserva wines of Vecchia Cantina, the co-operative of the zone, which groups together the harvest of some 300 small growers.

In Montepulciano's Piazza Grande, an open, irregularly shaped square at the top of the town, stands the Palazzo Contucci, opposite the crenellated rustic-looking Palazzo Comunale. One of the most interesting buildings in the town, the cellars beneath the palace house Contucci's winery, a fascinating place to wander through. It was completely renovated in the mid-1980s, and although still using traditional oak *botte*, the wines have a modern feel to them, with plenty of concentrated fruit. Contucci's wines can be tasted and purchased here, while other producers, including Poliziano and Del Cerro, two of the zone's leading lights, operate *vendite dirette* in the Piazza.

Map illustrations: (above left) the church of San Biagio; (above right) the Marzocco, symbol of medieval Florentine rule.

The Wine Country

Montepulciano's wine country extends over the flank of hills to the north and east of the town. Although this is an ancient wine zone, it has recently become one of Tuscany's more dynamic, with new investment bringing far-reaching changes. As in Chianti Classico there is a greater emphasis on Sangiovese and new plantings of Merlot and Cabernet, which frequently find expression in barrique-aged super-Tuscans. The more traditional blend of Sangiovese (here called Prugnolo Gentile) with Canaiolo and Mammolo has not been entirely abandoned – many estates both old and new use these grapes for Vino Nobile, still aged in large oak *botte*. Most importantly, the finest wines have benefited from improved vinification of better-quality grapes, increasingly sourced from vineyards planted with superior clones at higher densities.

Leave Montepulciano in the direction of Chianciano Terme, a once-stylish spa town famous for the efficacy of its waters – a good place for those who have overindulged (its motto is *fegato sano*, or healthy liver). At Sant'Albino, a winding lane to the left leads to the small 9ha estate of Le Casalte, originally begun as a hobby by the Barioffi family in the 1970s, and now the source of excellent Vino Nobile, the wines clarified with beaten egg white, the bottles even labelled by hand.

These newly planted vines are trained up canes for support; in the distance is the spa town of Chianciano Terme.

Head back in the direction of Montepulciano before turning right toward Argiano, a road that becomes an unpaved track leading across the flank of hills down toward the Chiana Valley. Woods soon give way to vineyards leading to Del Cerro, owned by the insurance company Saiagricola and the largest private estate in the Montepulciano zone, with 140ha of vineyards under cultivation. Cerro's pink Villa Grazianella, a majestic structure dating from the 15th century, stands above the ultra-modern winery of the estate. Further along the road is the young but dynamic Swiss-owned Terre Bindella, whose wines are now some of the best in the zone.

As the road descends to the flatter lands of the valley, vines give way to wheat and sunflowers. Turn left onto the S326 to Acquaviva, or detour right to the Lago di Montepulciano, a wildlife reserve that makes a nice spot for a picnic. Just outside Acquaviva, a typical farming community which boasts an excellent *trattoria*, L'Angelo, is the Boscarelli estate, whose finest wines are considered by many to be the purest and most typical expressions of Vino Nobile di Montepulciano; 'Boscarelli' is a polished super-Tuscan from pure Sangiovese aged in barrique.

Return to Acquaviva, crossing the S326 and the flat Chiana Valley to Valiano, where the ground begins to rise again. This medieval hill village is the centre for a handful of superlative wine estates. Trerose is one of the most modern wineries in the zone, with impressive state-of-the-art vinification and aging facilities. The Vino Nobile is produced in a style that is more international in character than traditional, while barrique-aged whites from Chardonnay, Sauvignon and Viognier are sleek and classy. The winery can be visited, although wines are not usually available for tasting.

Doubling back a short way through the village of Petrignano leads to Ruffino's Lodola Nuova estate, while Avignonesi's Le Capezzine estate is located further north beyond Trerose, toward Cortona Here, selected Sangiovese grapes are hung up to dry for the production of one of Italy's rarest and most highly sought after wines, Occhio di Pernice Vin Santo.

Return to Valiano, then recross the Chiana Valley through Montepulciano Stazione, a rather dull and dreary village, to Gracciano. Poliziano's handsome, modern *cantina* is located just before the village, a fitting home for this leading producer's sleek, modern and well-made wines. In addition to good Vino Nobile di Montepulciano, notably the Riservas Vigna Asinone and Vigna Caggiole, try either of the excellent super-Tuscans: Cabernet Le Stanze or Sangiovese Elegia. The La Braccesca estate, located along the provincial road, is a recent addition to the Antinori fold: quality is already promising, so no doubt this will be one estate to watch.

Montepulciano's wine country is lush and expansive, and provides wonderful views across its gently undulating hills.

Other estates in or around Gracciano include Fassati, which (with help from top enologist Franco Bernabei) has succeeded in a rapid transformation of its wines; and Fattoria di Gracciano, a producer of solid, traditional wines. From Gracciano, continue back to Montepulciano, or else make a detour first to Montefollonico, a small walled hill hamlet, home of small winegrower Vittorio Innocenti, as well as one of Tuscany's most famous restaurants, La Chiusa.

Returning to Montepulciano, the immense co-operative wine facilities of Vecchia Cantina are passed on the route back into town. Immediately on entering Montepulciano, find the road left that leads past the sports complex to Martiena, where, at Villa Martiena, the Dei estate produces wines of real character and quality. The Villa was remodelled at the turn of this century, while the modern winery, stunningly beautiful with its Travertino marble floor, is extremely well-equipped and up-to-date.

From Montepulciano, nearby Pienza is an easy drive. Considered the ideal Renaissance town, it was designed in 1459 at the request of Pope Pius II by the Florentine architect Bernardo Rossellino. There are opportunities for wine-tasting and buying in Pienza, as well as for buying the *pecorino* cheeses for which the area is justly famous.

Montepulciano Fact File

Despite the success of its wine production, Montepulciano sees relatively few visitors, and therefore makes an excellent base for the whole of southern Tuscany.

Information

There is an information office in Montepulciano on Via Ricci 7. Pienza's information office is in its main square, Piazza Pio II.

APT
Via G. Sabatini 7, 53042 Chianciano Terme. Tel 0578/63538; fax 0578/64623.

Consorzio del Vino Nobile di Montepulciano
Via delle Case Nuove 15, 53045 Montepulciano SI. Tel 0578/757812; fax 0578/758213.

Terre Toscane
Via del Teatro 19, 53045 Montepulciano SI. Tel 0578/758582; fax 0578/757098.
Agency for visits to producers, wine tastings and meals.

Markets

Montepulciano – Thursday
Pienza – Saturday

Festivals and Events

Montepulciano's wine festival, the *Bravío delle Botti*, takes place on the last Sunday in August. Men from the 8 *contrade* (quarters) of the town compete to push barrels uphill for the length of the Corso. Local food specialities are available.

During the *Cantine Aperte*, usually in mid-May, the town celebrates 'open cellars' day with a sign-posted city centre walk.

Enoteche and Bars

In Montepulciano itself most shops offer wines, and some producers have their own outlets in the town.

Enoteca Baccus
Corso Rossellino 105, 53026 Pienza SI.
Small and friendly, with a good range of wines, as well as exceptional *grappe* by the glass.

Enoteche Oinochóe
Via di Voltaia nel Corso 82, 53045 Montepulciano SI.

The best independent wine shop: wines from all the zone's finest producers are available for tasting.

Antico Caffè Poliziano
Via di Voltaia nel Corso 27-29, 53045 Montepulciano SI.
Magnificent old-world *caffè* with a fine selection of Vino Nobile and excellent coffee and pastries.

Enoteca Lo Strettoio
Piazza Pasquino 1, 53045 Montepulciano SI.
Wines from 3 small, respected local growers – La Casella, Tiberini and Vittorio Innocente.

Where to Stay and Eat

Locanda dell'Amorosa Ⓗ Ⓡ
Loc. L'Amorosa, 53048 Sinalunga SI. Tel 0577/679497; fax 0577/678216. Ⓛ Ⓛ Ⓛ
One of the most famous restaurants in Tuscany. Refined but genuine country dishes.

Trattoria L'Angolo Ⓗ Ⓡ
Via G. Galilei 20, 53040 Acquaviva SI. Tel 0578/767216. Ⓛ
This family-run *trattoria* is the best in the wine country: good local food, as well as two *menu di degustazione* that include wines; pizza in the evening. Two mini-apartments for rent.

Albergo Il Borghetto Ⓗ
Via Borgo Buio 7, 53045 Montepulciano SI. Tel 0578/757535. Ⓛ Ⓛ
Atmospheric small hotel with 11 rooms built into the town walls.

Trattoria La Buca delle Fate Ⓡ
Corso Rossellino 38a, 53026 Pienza SI. Tel 0578/748448. Ⓛ
Pienza's most reliable restaurant; good selection of local wines.

Ristorante Il Cantuccio Ⓡ
Via delle Cantine 1-2, 53045 Montepulciano SI. Tel 0578/757870. Ⓛ

Atmospheric vaulted restaurant serving traditional food and a range of local wines.

La Chiusa Ⓗ Ⓡ
Via della Madonnina 88, 53040 Montefollonico SI. Tel 0577/669668; fax 0577/669593.
Ⓛ Ⓛ Ⓛ
Famous, elegant and very expensive restaurant, with rooms, in an ancient farmhouse. Serves refined Tuscan as well as *cucina creativa*. Extensive wine list.

Trattoria Diva e Maceo Ⓡ
Via di Gracciano nel Corso 36, 53045 Montepulciano SI. Tel 0578/716951. Ⓛ
Good *trattoria* for homecooked local food and wines.

Ristorante/Enoteca La Grotta Ⓡ
Loc. San Biagio 15, 53045 Montepulciano SI. Tel 0578/757607. Ⓛ Ⓛ
The best restaurant in town, serving traditional food with care and style. The large wine list is excellent; wines can be purchased from the *enoteca*.

Albergo Il Marzocco Ⓗ
Piazza Savonarola 18, 53045 Montepulciano SI. Tel 0578/757262; fax 0578/757530. Ⓛ Ⓛ
Comfortable, large, airy rooms in a 3-star hotel located in a 16th-century palace; some have terraces with panoramic views.

Agriturismo

Borgo delle More
Via de Montenero 18, 53040 Acquaviva SI. Tel 0578/768166; fax 0578/767798.
Well-reconstructed *agriturismo* complex in the heart of the wine country. Apartments, barbeque area and large swimming pool.

Borgo Trerose Ⓗ
Loc. I Palazzi, 53040 Valiano SI. Tel 0578/724231; fax 0578/724227.
Luxury complex in a medieval *borgo* attached to the Tenuta Trerose wine estate. Well-renovated apartments, rooms in the hotel. Swimming pool.

Wines and Wine Villages

Outside Montepulciano itself, interest is restricted to an even spread of often welcoming wine estates found on the gentle slopes.

Abbadia and Ascianello

Adjoining *frazioni* in the north of the commune with some important vineyards sites

Bianco Vergine Valdichiana

DOC   Mostly uninteresting dry whites based on Trebbiano and, to a lesser extent, Malvasia, although Manzano makes an acceptable one. Some producers have opted to dry the grapes for Vin Santo or have added something better to sell it as vino da tavola with a *nome da fantasia*.

Caggiole and Cervognano

Typical mid-altitude slopes running away from Montepulciano down to the Chiana Valley and resulting in good-quality wines.

Chianti dei Colli Senesi

DOCG   Light, easy-drinking wine, usually from vines outside the Montepulciano zone. Better examples come from Castello di Farnetella at Sinalunga.
Best producers: *Burrachi*, DEL CERRO, *Gracciano, Vittorio Innocenti*, POLIZIANO.
See also p.49.

Gracciano   Small town that is

the centre for a number of producers; the surrounding *frazione* contains some well-sited vineyards.

Montefollonico   Quiet

fortified medieval village and an adjoining commune to Montepulciano. Vittorio Innocenti has vines on both sides of the boundary – only a small amount qualifies as Vino Nobile.

Montepulciano   Renaissance

wine town containing wonderful palaces, churches and cellars. From its highest point (665m/2180ft) in the west, the ridge on which this noble city sits runs north and eastwards, ever lower and flatter toward the Chiana Valley, its

Vino Nobile is at last living up to its name. Watch out, too, for good-value Rossi di Montepulciano.

flanks covered with vines. There is more sand (mixed with clay) here than in Chianti Classico or Montalcino, but this does not seem to affect this zone's potential.

As in Chianti Classico, the limitations of the Vino Nobile regulations have forced a number of the more progressive producers to produce super-Tuscans. These are usually based on Sangiovese, in many instances 100 per cent; others add Cabernet or Merlot. Most are aged in new oak.
Best producers: *(Sangiovese super-Tuscans)* BINDELLA, BOSCARELLI, POLIZIANO, *Romeo, Sant'Agnese, Sant'Anna*.

Rosso di Montepulciano

DOC   Introduced as recently as 1989 this is intended as a second wine from young vines or from those less suitable for Vino Nobile. Though not made by all producers and not yet a match for Rosso di Montalcino, it can nevertheless be a vibrant, fruity early-drinking wine that helps preserve the quality of Vino Nobile – and improves a producer's cash flow.
Best producers: AVIGNONESI, BOSCARELLI, *La Braccesca, Buracchi*, LE CASALTE, DEL CERRO, *Contucci*, POLIZIANO, *Valdipiatta*

Sant'Albino   Only two

important producers, Le Casalte and Paterno, are based here but the vineyards lie at 400–500m (1300–1650ft) on well-sited gentle slopes.

Valiano   A small town and

frazione – an isolated area of higher land across the lowest part of the Chiana Valley. Avignonesi's Le Cappezzine estate is here, as are Tenuta Trerose, La Calonica and Ruffino-managed Lodola Nuova.

Vino Nobile di Montepulciano DOCG   For a

long time this was anything but a 'noble wine'. Despite historic evidence for a longer, more continuous tradition of fine wine than its dynamic neighbour Montalcino, its true potential remained unrealized.

The granting of the DOCG in 1981 (and its revision in 1989) has had a positive influence, as has the worldwide revolution in wine-making. Most importantly, committed individuals, aided by super-enologists such as Maurizio Castelli and Vittorio Fiore, have brought about much needed changes – the results of which have been most evident from the 1990 vintage onward.

Wines show something of the weight, power and warmth of Brunello, but a handful of examples also exhibit the exquisite class seen in the best Sangiovese-based wines from Chianti Classico and Rufina.

The DOCG regulations stipulate a maximum of 80% Sangiovese (known locally as Prugnolo Gentile), although this is ignored by some. Canaiolo and the fragrant Mammolo and, before 1989, white grapes make up the rest of the blend.
Best producers: AVIGNONESI, BINDELLA, BOSCARELLI, *La Braccesca, Canneto*, LE CASALTE, *La Casella, Contucci, Dei*, DEL CERRO, FASSATI, *Gracciano, Vittorio Innocenti, Il Macchione, Paterno, Poggio alla Sala*, POLIZIANO, *Sant'Anna*, TREROSE, *Valdipiatta*.

A-Z of Main Wine Producers

The decline of the *mezzadria* system (share cropping) in the 1950s and 60s, together with the switch from mixed cultivation to monoculture, coincided with the huge commercial success of basic Chianti. Production in the 1960s and 70s came to be dominated by large merchant houses. But the Italian wine-making revolution of the 1980s, combined with outside investment, has assisted the rise of the small, independent producer, whose success has encouraged even those with tiny holdings to bottle the wine themselves. The following is a selection of the leading producers in the region.

Key to Symbols

Visiting arrangements ⊘ Visitors welcome ⊘ By appointment
Ⓧ No visitors.
Wine styles made ⓲ Red wine ⓤ White wine ⓤ Rosé wine.
Page numbers refer to the tour featuring the producer.

Altesino
Loc. Altesino, frazione Torrenieri, 53028 Montalcino SI. Tel 0577/806208; fax 0577/806131. ⊘⓲ⓤ pp.52, 56, 63
Considered one of the modern school of Brunello, with intense concentrated wines, but it is often only the Cru Montosoli that really combines elegance with power. The barrique-aged Sangiovese, Palazzo Altesi, is consistently fine; the other super-Tuscan, Alte Altesi, is a blend of Sangiovese and Cabernet. There is also some good Rosso di Montalcino.

Antinori
Piazza degli Antinori 3, 50123 Florence. Tel 055/2359848; fax 055/2359877. Ⓧ⓲ⓤⓤ pp.8, 26-8, 30, 42, 52, 53, 69
Perhaps Tuscany's foremost representative, the Marchese Piero Antinori, and now his 3 daughters, continue to advance the cause of Italian wine. The famous Tignanello and Solaia from the Santa Cristina estate are the leaders of a considerable

array of wines, including Tenute Marchesi and Badia a Passignano Chianti Classicos and Guado al Tasso from Bolgheri. There are enterprises in Montalcino and Montepulciano, but the wine-making is in San Casciano in the north of the Classico zone. Quality at the lower levels is consistent but less exciting.

Ambra
Via Lombarda 85, 50042 Carmignano PO. Tel 055/486488. ⊘⓲ pp.16, 18
Small but quality-orientated producer Giuseppe Rigoli continues to refine Carmignano, especially the Cru versions.

Argiano
Frazione Sant'Angelo in Colle, 53020 Montalcino SI. Tel 0577/864037; fax 0577/864210. ⊘⓲ pp.59, 62, 63
This estate is a new star that will continue to rise. Real changes have been made here since the Contessa Noema Marone Cinzano took control in 1992. Winemaker Sebastiano Rosa (who formerly spent time at Sassicaia), aided by Giacomo Tachis, has begun to transform these wines into some of the most modern in the zone. Brunello and Brunello Riserva are partly aged in new oak and already show supremely concentrated ripe fruit.

Artimino
Loc. Artimino, 50042 Carmignano PO. Tel 055/8792051. ⊘⓲ pp.16, 18
Carmignano's largest producer, with more than 80ha. Its reputation has been forged around the Carmignano Riserva Villa Medicea, but the entire range is beginning to benefit from new investment.

Avignonesi
Via di Gracciano del Corso 91, 53040 Montepulciano SI. Tel 0578/757872; fax 0578/757847. ⊘⓲ⓤ pp.8, 66, 69, 71
Montepulciano's long-standing leading producer. A quality-first, innovative approach has made the name synonymous with the zone. Ettore Falvo fashioned some of Tuscany's first varietals from Chardonnay (Il Marzocco) Sauvignon (Il Vignola) and Merlot. Grifi, the 50-50 Sangiovese-Cabernet, is the best known, but one wine is a world apart – the outstanding rare Vin Santo Occhio di Pernice, made from Sangiovese (Prugnolo) – while the white Vin Santo from Grechetto remains a classic.

Bacchereto
Via Fontemorana 179, Loc. Bacchereto, 50040 Carmignano PO. Tel & fax 055/8717191. ⊘⓲ⓤ pp.17, 18
The production of olive oil and honey are almost as important as the wines on this friendly estate.

Badia a Coltibuono
Loc. Badia a Coltibuono, 53013 Gaiole in Chianti SI. Tel 0577/749300; fax 0577/749235. ⊘⓲ⓤ pp.31, 41
This isolated historic estate has most of its vineyards to the south, at Monti in Chianti, but there is consistently good quality across the range. Three wines stand out – the standard Chianti Classico, the Riserva version and the barrique-aged Sangiovese called Sangioveto, which is very good. Cetamura, previously Chianti Classico but now of much wider origin, is still good value for money.

Banfi
Loc. Sant'Angelo Scalo, 53020
Montalcino SI. Tel 0577/840111;
fax 0577/840444. ⊘🕐🕑
pp.59–60, 62, 63
Overseen by the renowned Ezio
Rivella, this is the giant of
Montalcino. The impressive
winery draws from 800ha of
vines, planted mostly at low
altitudes, though the estate
includes the higher vineyard of
Poggio all'Oro, the source of the
impressive Riserva. Premium
varietals and an everyday range
come from Cabernet Sauvignon,
Merlot, Syrah, Pinot Nero,
Chardonnay and Sauvignon.
Summus, unusually, combines
Sangiovese with Cabernet and
Syrah. Rosso di Montalcino and
Moscadello are also good.

Barbi
Loc. Podernovi 170, 53024
Montalcino SI. Tel 0577/848277;
fax 0577/849356. ⊘🕐 pp.58,
62, 63
Francesca Colombini Cinelli,
who started the Movimento del
Turismo del Vino, and her
daughter Donatella run this
welcoming estate. Vigna del
Fiore Riserva is the best of the 3
much-improved Brunellos.

Bindella
Via delle Tre Berte 10A, 53040
Montepulciano SI. Tel 0578/
767777; fax 0578/767255. ⊘🕐
pp.68, 71
Tenuta Vallocaia, the property of
Swiss importer Rudi Bindella, is

an excellent source of Vino
Nobile and Vino Nobile Riserva.
Vittorio Fiore consults here and,
as elsewhere, his touch is sure –
even in a difficult vintage such as
1992 the Vino Nobile is fine.
Consistently good, too, is the
oak-aged super-Tuscan from
Sangiovese, Vallocaia.

Biondi-Santi
Loc. Greppo, 53024 Montalcino
SI. Tel 0577/847121; fax 0577/
848087 ⊘🕐🕑 pp.58, 62, 63
The most renowned producer in
Tuscany, yet recently much
criticized. The Riserva is
legendary, with tremendous
extract, tannin and acidity, and
should be broached only after at
least a decade. Brunello was not
created here, but Biondi-Santi
was most certainly responsible
for its renown. These very
expensive wines remain a style
apart, requiring long aging to
reveal, from certain vintages,
true greatness.

Boscarelli
Via di Montecuo 28, Loc.
Cervognano, 53045
Montepulciano SI. Tel 0578/
767277; fax 0578/767650. ⊘🕐
pp.8, 68, 71
The vineyards around
Cervognano are some of the best
in the zone, and star enologist
Maurizio Castelli adds technical
brilliance to the family's
commitment and hard work.
Now, arguably, the single best
producer of Vino Nobile – even
in difficult years it rarely
disappoints, and the Riserva is
even better; Riserva del Nocio is
a more specific selection. The
only super-Tuscan, Boscarelli, is
an excellent barrique-aged
Sangiovese; the Rosso di
Montepulciano is good.

Buonamico
Via Provinciale di Montecarlo
43, Loc. Cercatoia, 55015
Montecarlo LU. Tel & fax
0583/22038. ⊘🕐🕑
Vasco Grassi's excellent estate,
like others here, benefits from an
interesting grape mix. Rosso di
Cercatoia (Sangiovese dominant),
Il Fortino Cabernet-Merlot and
Il Fortino Syrah are the top reds.
The characterful white Bianco di
Cercatoia contains Trebbiano,
Pinot Bianco, Pinot Grigio,
Sauvignon Blanc and Sémillon;
the even better Vasario is based
on Pinot Bianco.

Canalicchio di Sotto
Podere Canalicchio di Sotto 8,
53024 Montalcino SI. Tel
0577/848476; fax 0577/848476.
⊘🕐 pp.57, 62, 63
Maurizio Lambardi makes an
outstanding trio of reds – Rosso,
Brunello and Brunello Riserva –
in very small quantities.

Capaccia
Loc. Capaccia, 53017 Radda in
Chianti SI. Tel 0574/582426; fax
0574/582428. ⊘🕐🕑 pp.31, 42
High hill vineyards and
meticulous care in the cellar
under consultant Vittorio Fiore
result in Querciagrande, and
outstanding barrique-aged super-
Tuscan Sangiovese.

Caparzo
Loc. Torrenieri, 53028
Montalcino SI. Tel 0577/
848390; fax 0577/849377.
⊘🕐🕑 pp.56, 62, 63
One of Montalcino's best
producers. The partly barrique-
aged Brunello La Casa from the
Montosoli vineyard is one of the
zone's great wines, despite some
criticism of recent vintages. Le
Grance was one of the first

predominantly Chardonnay wines in Tuscany and is now a confirmed star. Also good are Brunello normale, the Rosso di Montalcino and Sangiovese-Cabernet Cà del Pazzo.

Capezzana
Via di Capezzana 100, Loc. Seano, 50042 Carmignano PO. Tel 055/8706005; fax 055/8706673. ⊘◉⊕◉ pp.16, 17, 18
This splendid estate has come to epitomize the Carmignano zone. Count Ugo Contini Bonacossi quietly continues to advance its reputation with the aristocratic Carmignano Riserva and balanced, harmonious Villa di Trefiano. Barco Reale and Vin Ruspo originated here and become ever more stylish everyday wines. Vin Santo is concentrated and particularly refined, its dried- and candied-fruit flavours becoming more nutty and honeyed with age.

Casale-Falchini
Via di Casale 40, 53037 San Gimignano SI. Tel 0577/941305; fax 0577/37204. ⊘⊕◉ pp.46, 49
Riccardo Falchini first gets the best out of Vernaccia, then shows what else San Gimignano is capable of. Red wines are particularly successful. The best is Campora, a Cabernet Sauvignon with Sangiovese, although the Sangiovese Paretaio is also good. Very good Chianti dei Colli Senesi, Vin Santo, a decent Chardonnay (Capitolare del Muschio) and the sparkling Falchini Brut show the depth of this producer's range.

Casanova di Neri
Podere Casanova, Loc. Torrenieri, 53028 Montalcino SI. Tel 0577/834029; fax 0577/834455. ⊘◉ pp.52, 62, 63
Anything from Giacomo Neri's estate is worth a try, but expect the Brunello to be an intense,

concentrated wine that needs to be cellared. This and the Riserva Cerretalto are likely to become classics; the Rosso is a good buy.

Le Casalte
Via del Termine 2, Sant'Albino, 53045 Montepulciano SI. Tel 0578/799138; fax 06/9306988. ⊘◉⊕◉ pp.68, 71
Guido Barioffi is an excellent small producer. The care lavished on the well-sited vines is evident in the quality of the fruit. With expert consultant wine-making, Vino Nobile and Vino Nobile Riserva are often near the best in the zone, and the vibrant, fruity Rosso for early drinking is good value.

Case Basse
Loc. Villa Santa Restituta, 53024 Montalcino SI. Tel 0577/848567. ⊘◉ pp.60, 62
From low-yielding vines in one of Montalcino's best sites, this estate earned a reputation in the 1980s as one of the zone's handful of top producers. Owner Gianfranco Soldera and master consultant Giulio Gambelli are likely to retain this status, given the performance of the Riserva in 1983, 85, 88 and 90. Intistieti is essentially the same wine as the Brunello but spends less time in the traditional oak *botte*.

Castellare di Castellina
Loc. Castellare, 53011 Castellina in Chianti SI. Tel & fax 0577/740490. ⊘◉⊕ pp.34, 40
Consistent quality estate, long aided by enologist Maurizio Castelli. Fine Chianti Classico and Riserva are produced from stony soils. The best-known wine is I Sodi di San Niccolò – its distinctive dark flavours and perfume derived in part from 10 per cent Malvasia Nera added to the Sangiovese. Good Cabernet (Coniale), Chardonnay (Canonico) and Sauvignon (Spartito).

Castelli del Grevepesa
Via Grevigiana 34, Loc. Ponte di Gabbiano, 50024 San Casciano Val di Pesa FI. Tel 055/821101; fax 055/8217920. ⊘◉ pp.28, 42
A number of Chianti labels, including Castelgreve, Clemente

VII and Montefiridolfi, emerge from this co-operative that sources its grapes from growers in the northern half of the Classico zone. Quality is fair, but it is reasonable value.

Castell'in Villa
Loc. Castell'in Villa, 53019 Castelnuovo Berardenga SI. Tel 0577/359074; fax 0577/359222. ⊘◉ pp.33, 40
The reputation of this fine estate is founded primarily on Chianti Classico and Riserva, which are intense and long-lived. Recent changes have had some impact, with one or two misses as the wines become more streamlined. Good Vin Santo and a barrique-aged Sangiovese, Santa Croce.

Castello dei Rampolla
Santa Lucia in Faulle, frazione Panzano, 50020 Greve in Chianti FI. Tel 055/852001; fax 055/852533. ⊘◉ pp.8, 29, 42
Home to Sammarco, the great Cabernet Sauvignon of the Panzano hills, created by Alceo di Napoli. This estate is now run by Luca and Maurizia di Napoli, with Giacomo Tachis advising. Chianti Classico and Riserva, which benefit from Cabernet in the blend, are also stylish.

Castello di Ama
Loc. Ama, frazione Lecchi in Chianti, 53010 Gaiole in Chianti SI. Tel 0577/746031; fax 0577/746117. ⊘◉⊕ p.8, 33, 41
This superbly situated estate continues to improve its already impressive wines. The Vigna l'Apparita Merlot is one of the most profound of all super-Tuscans; single-vineyard *Crus* Bellavista and La Casuccia are both superb Chianti Classico. The Pinot Nero Vigna Il Chiuso looks increasingly exciting, as do the very good whites: Vigna Al Poggio (Chardonnay) and Vigna Bellaria (Pinot Grigio).

Castello di Brolio
Loc. Brolio, 53013 Gaiole in Chianti SI. Tel 0577/749066. ⊘◉⊕ pp.32, 41
It has been a long time since the wines matched the grandeur of the castle itself, but the return of

ownership to the Ricasoli family promises much. With help from Filippo Mazzei of Fonterutoli and enologist Carlo Ferrini, the wines are already radically improved. The Ricasoli label denotes a more basic range.

Castello di Cacchiano
Loc. Monti in Chianti, 53010 Gaiole in Chianti SI. Tel 0577/747018; fax 055/216529. ✓ ● ① pp.33, 41
Sometimes criticized for their rusticity, the wines here include full, fruity and robust Chianti Classico. Plantings of Merlot and Malvasia Nera are intended to replace the 10 per cent Canaiolo that currently complements the Sangiovese in most reds.

Castello di Querceto
frazione Dudda, Lucolena, 50020 Greve in Chianti FI. Tel 055/8549064; fax 055/8549063. ✓ ● pp.28, 41
Accessible wines from this out-of-the-way estate. The quality found in Chianti Classico, Riserva and Riserva Il Pichio is reinforced by super-Tuscans Cignale (Cabernet with 10 per cent Merlot), La Corte (Sangiovese) and Querciolaia (Sangiovese-Cabernet).

Castello di Verrazzano
Loc. Castello di Verrazzano, 50022 Greve in Chianti FI. Tel 055/854243; fax 055/854241. ✓ ● ① pp.28, 41
Commercially orientated but quality estate noted for 2 barrique-aged Sangioveses: Bottiglia Particolare and Sassello.

Castello di Vicchiomaggio
Via Vicchiomaggio 4, 50022 Greve in Chianti FI. Tel 055/854079; fax 055/853911. ✓ ● pp.28, 41
John Matta's estate may not be top flight, but wines such as Chianti Classico San Jacopo, more concentrated Petri Riserva, and

the intense and vibrant La Prima Riserva are attractive and accessible. Super-Tuscan Ripa delle More lacks intensity.

Castello di Volpaia
Loc. Volpaia, 53017 Radda in Chianti SI. Tel 0577/738066; fax 0577/738619. ✓ ● ① pp.29, 31, 42
Wines of real refinement from one of Chianti's prettiest and highest hilltop hamlets. Under consultant Maurizio Castelli, the range runs from the long-established Sangiovese-based super-Tuscans Coltassala (with a little Mammolo) and Balifico (with Cabernet Sauvignon and Cabernet Franc) through excellent Chianti Classico and Riserva to a good dry white, Torniella (predominantly Sauvignon), and Vin Santo.

Cecchi
Loc. Casina dei Ponti 53011 Castellina in Chianti SI. Tel 0577/743024; fax 0577/743057. ✓ ● p.40
The well-known producer is often associated with decent basic Chianti, but Villa Cerna wines are a solidly consistent step up. Noteworthy, too, are Chianti Classico Messer Pietro di Teuzzo and Spargolo, an oak-aged Sangiovese.

Cerbaiona
Loc. Cerbaiona, 53024 Montalcino SI. Tel & fax 0577/848660. ✓ ● pp.58, 62
One of Montalcino's many tiny producers, Diego Molinari makes Brunello second to none and an earlier-bottled and earlier-drinking Cerbaiona.

Del Cerro
Via Grazianella 5, frazione Acquaviva, 53040 Montepulciano SI. Tel 0578/767722; fax 0578/768040. ✓ ● ① pp.58, 67, 68, 71
Following improvements in the vineyard and winery, this large producer is gaining a reputation for Vino Nobile and Vino Nobile Riserva. Rosso di Montepulciano is one of the best, and the white blend Thesis shows promise.

Ciacci Piccolomini d'Aragona
Via Borgo di Mezzo 62, frazione Castelnuovo dell'Abate, 53020 Montalcino SI. Tel 0577/835616; fax 0577/835785. ✓ ● pp.59, 62, 63
Arresting quality here owes much to Roberto Cipresso. The Brunello Vigna di Pianrosso is powerful, concentrated and beautifully balanced – the 1988 and 90 are outstanding. The Rosso di Montalcino Vigna della Fonte is also good, as is the partially barrique-aged Ateo.

Col d'Orcia
Frazione Sant'Angelo in Colle, 53024 Montalcino SI. Tel 0577/808001; fax 0577/864018. ✓ ● ① pp.60, 62, 63
Large Cinzano-owned property producing good Brunello, although it is the Riserva Poggio al Vento that really sings. The potential for Cabernet is shown here in Olmaia, and Chardonnay Ghiaie Bianche shows promise. Rosso di Montalcino scores highly for value and drinkability. There is excellent sweet Moscadello di Montalcino (Vendemmia Tardiva Pascena).

Costanti
Loc. Colle al Matrichese, 53024 Montalcino SI. Tel 0577/848195; fax 0577/849349. ✗ ● pp.57, 58, 62, 63
The Colle al Matrichese of Andrea Costanti is based on vineyards on the same ridge as those of Biondi-Santi but it also includes a small plot in Montosoli. The wines are impeccable but need several years to show at their best. Brunello is consistently fine, and the Riserva is destined to be a classic. The Rosso can be intense and closed when young but is excellent after 5 years or so. Vermiglio is round and almost immediately drinkable.

Dei
Villa Martiena, Via di Martiena 35, 53045 Montepulciano SI. Tel 0578/716878; fax 0577/704275. ⊘● pp.69, 71
The Dei family have been making wines here only since 1985, but impressive Vino Nobile, Riserva and, lately, Rosso show what can be achieved with investment and the consultancy of Niccolò d'Afflitto.

Dievole
53010 Vagliagli SI. Tel 0577/ 322613; fax 0577/322574. ⊘● pp.35, 42
Mario Schwenn offers a warm welcome. His numerous Chianti Classicos can all be remarkably good, well-priced wines, especially the Villa Dievole.

Fassati
Via di Graccianello 3A, Loc. Gracciano, 53040 Montepulciano SI. Tel 0578/ 708708; fax 0578/708705. ⊘●⊕⊕ pp.69, 71
Owned by Verdicchio producer Fazi Battaglia. Substantial investment in the vineyards, the direction of Amedeo Esposito, and consultancy of enologist Franco Bernabei have all boosted quality, most appreciable in vintages since 1991. Both Vino Noble and Riserva have added richness, freshness and better structure. Spigo is a rare and delightful rosé.

Felsina Berardenga
Strada Chiantigiana 484, 53019 Castelnuovo Berardenga SI. Tel 0577/355117; fax 0577/355651. ⊘●⊕ pp.8, 33, 40
Now one of Chianti Classico's leading names. Giuseppe Mazzocolin and consultant Franco Bernabei make a formidable range of wines. Much emphasis is placed on bold and meaty Chianti Classico. The Riserva adds depth, and Riserva Vigneto Rancia is complex and ageworthy. Maestro Raro is a Cabernet-based super-Tuscan, but the real star of this producer is the barrique-aged Sangiovese, Fontalloro, a deep, powerful and beautifully made wine – one of Tuscany's best.

White wines include the ripe and oaky Chardonnay, I Sistri, while a sweet Vin Santo has recently been released for the first time.

Fonterutoli
Loc. Fonterutoli, 53011 Castellina in Chianti SI. Tel 0577/740476; fax 0577/741070. ⊘●⊕ pp.8, 35, 40
Filippo Mazzei's family have owned this estate since 1435. Currently 60ha out of a total 444ha are planted to vines. Three wines stand out: Ser Lapo is the Chianti Classico Riserva; Concerto is oak-aged Sangiovese with 20 per cent Cabernet; and the exciting Siepi is Sangiovese and 20 per cent Merlot. The Chardonnay-based Fontestella is a new addition.

Fontodi
Via San Leolino 37, frazione Panzano, 50020 Greve in Chianti FI. Tel 055/852005; fax 055/852537. ⊘●⊕ pp.8, 29, 42
Model estate on Panzano's golden slopes. The wines are consistent and show real finesse. Chianti Classico is fine, the Riserva and Riserva Vigna del Sorbo add more depth and structure. Flaccianello has been one of the finest pure Sangiovese wines for well over a decade. Young vines yield good Pinot Nero and Syrah under the name Case Via. The white Meriggio is based on Pinot Bianco.

Frescobaldi
Via Santo Spirito 11, 50125 Florence. Tel 055/2381400; fax 055/8363077. ⊘●⊕ pp.19, 21, 23, 60, 63
The 8 estates of Frescobaldi total more than 850ha of vineyards. Large volumes of an acceptable red Chianti Remole are produced at Poggio a Remole, and from Nipozzano come 2 of Tuscany's most ageworthy wines: Chianti Rufina Riserva and the often majestic Montesodi. Tenuta di Pomino is best known for the white Il Benefizio from high, cool vineyards. In the warm south at Tenuta di Castelgiocondo in Montalcino, good Brunello and better Riserva are produced, as well as reliable Rosso di Montalcino Campo ai Sassi and an inviting Merlot, Lamaione. There will also be a new enterprise in Tuscany with California's Robert Mondavi.

Grattamacco
Loc. Grattamacco, 57022 Castagneto Carducci LI. Tel & fax 0565/763840. ⊘●⊕ pp.52, 53
Piermario Melitti Cavallari makes only one red and one white. Grattamacco Rosso, a blend of Cabernet Sauvignon, Sangiovese and Merlot, looks set to keep pace with the best in Bolgheri. Grattamacco Bianco, half Trebbiano, half Vermentino is fresh and stylish.

Isole e Olena
Via Olena, Loc. Isole, 50021 Barberino Val d'Elsa FI. Tel 055/8072763; fax 055/8072236. ⊗●⊕ pp.8, 34, 40
Inspired, hard-working Paolo De Marchi leads by example – the transformation of an old-style estate to one in the upper ranks has been dramatic. Cepparello is one of the finest examples of pure Sangiovese, and there is impressive Cabernet and Syrah and a delectable Vin Santo. The Chianti Classico is marvellously consistent and one of the best.

Le Macchiole
Via Bolgherese 189a, 57020 Bolgheri LI. Tel & fax 0565/ 766092. ⊘●⊕⊕ pp.52, 53

The Campolmi family's small Bolgheri estate. Reduced yields and improvements in the winery are part of the relentless pursuit of quality. Both Paléo Rosso (Cabernet with 10 per cent Sangiovese) and Paléo Bianco (Chardonnay, Sauvignon and Vermentino) are now very good. Merlot is new and Le Contessine wines are lower-priced red, white and rosé.

Fattoria di Manzano
Via di Manzano 15, Loc. Camucia, 52042 Cortona AR. Tel 0575/618667; fax 0575/ 618411. ⊘⊕⊕
One of the best new names, but lying outside a major zone. Freedom from DOC constraints, together with massive investment, mean that quality is already high. Vigna del Bosco is pure Syrah, Le Terrazze is from Sauvignon, Podere di Fontarca combines Chardonnay with Viognier, and Vescovo is Gamay.

Mastrojanni
Podere Loreto, frazione Castelnuovo dell'Abate, 53020 Montalcino SI. Tel 0577/ 835681; fax 0577/835505. ⊘⊕ pp.59, 62, 63
Under enologist Maurizio Castelli the wines have taken on an extra dimension, further enhancing an already enviable reputation. Brunello includes Riserva and Cru Schiena d'Asino. San Pio is Sangiovese with 25 per cent Cabernet.

Melini
Frazione Gaggiano, 53036 Poggibonsi SI. Tel 0577/989001 ⊘⊕
Part of the giant Gruppo Italiano Vini (GIV), these widely available wines are inexpensive, and include Chianti Classico Isassi and Riserva La Selvanella, both of which can be remarkable value for money.

Monsanto
Via Monsanto 8 , 50021 Barberino Val d'Elsa FI. Tel 055/8059000; fax 055/8059000. ⊘⊕⊕ pp.35, 40
The wines from Fabrizio Bianchi's famous estate retain an

undiminished reputation for aging. Il Poggio Riserva is cited most often, but the pure Sangiovese, Fabrizio Bianchi, is equally noteworthy. Other powerful, complex reds include Tinscvil, a Sangiovese-Cabernet blend and the Cabernet Nemo. The Chardonnay can also be impressive.

Monte Bernardi
Via Chiantigiana, frazione Panzano, 50020 Greve in Chianti FI. Tel 055/852400; fax 055/852355. ⊘⊕ pp.29, 42
Dynamic estate on the most southern of Panzano's slopes producing small quantities of wine. Pure Sangiovese, whether in Chianti Classico or oaky super-Tuscan Sa'etta, rarely finds better expression, but there is also a brilliant Cabernet.

Montenidoli
Loc. Montenidoli, 53037 San Gimignano SI. Tel 0577/ 941565; fax 0577/942037. ⊘⊕⊕⊕ pp.47, 49
As well as a range of distinctive Vernaccia di San Gimignano, Elisabetta Fagiuoli and her daughter Angelica make an unusual rosé from Canaiolo called Canaiuolo. Sono Montenidoli is a lively red from Sangiovese and Malvasia Nera.

Montevertine
Loc. Montevertine, 53017 Radda in Chianti SI. Tel 0577/738009; fax 0577/738265. ⊘⊕⊕ pp.8, 30, 42
Historically important for making the first pure Sangiovese super-Tuscan, Le Pergole Torte. This wine remains one of Tuscany's best – little wonder when owner Sergio Manetti and his son Martino continue to work with master consultant Giulio Gambelli. Il Sodaccio and Montevertine Riserva, both with a percentage of Canaiolo, can also be outstanding.

Silvio Nardi
Loc. Casale del Bosco, 53024 Montalcino SI. Tel & fax 0577/808269. ⊘⊕ pp.62, 63
Significantly, the Brunello from this much-improved estate,

managed by Emilia Nardi, comes from the favoured south-east of the zone. Improvement is likely to continue, given increased vine density, lower yields, a new winery and a top consultant.

Tenuta dell'Ornellaia
Via Bolgherese 191, 57020 Bolgheri LI. Tel 0565/762140; fax 0565/762144. ✗⊕⊕ pp.8, 51, 53
The no-expense-spared winery at this quality estate produces wines of integrity and sheer class. The cult Merlot, Masseto, is likely to gain ever greater acclaim. The estate Ornellaia is already one of the world's best Cabernet-based wines, while vibrant pure Sauvignon Blanc (Poggio alle Gazze) combines the best of old world with that of the new.

Panizzi
Loc. Santa Margherita, 53037 San Gimignano SI. Tel & fax 0577/ 941576. ⊘⊕⊕ pp.47, 49
Although Giovanni Panizzi possesses only 6ha of vineyards, low yields, careful selection and intelligent consultant-assisted wine-making have quickly made him one of the zone's best producers. The wines are balanced, stylish, fresh and characterful. Unusually, the Vernaccia di San Gimignano Riserva shows some ability to age.

Pietraserena
Loc. Casale 5, 53037 San Gimignano SI. Tel 0577/ 940083; fax 0577/942045. ⊘⊕⊕⊕ pp.46, 47, 49
An improving producer. Vigna del Sole is a refined, concentrated Vernaccia; Caulio from Sangiovese is intense and structured; Merlot is a new addition; there is also a rosé and Vin Santo.

Pieve Santa Restituta
Loc. Chiesa di Santa Restituta, 53024 Montalcino SI. Tel 0577/848610; fax 0577/849309.
⊘🌢🍷 pp.60, 62
Gaja's first Tuscan venture is located in one of the zone's finest sites. New investment has added to the efforts of Roberto Bellini, and name changes with new wines are likely to follow. There may soon be Brunello here the like of which has never been seen before; also the source of the best Vin Santo in Italy.

Poggio Antico
Loc. I Poggi, 53024 Montalcino SI. Tel & fax 0577/848044.
⊘🌢 pp.60, 62, 63
Paola Gloder is widely respected for her estate's consistency and for her efforts to broaden the appeal of her wines. The vines are among the highest in the zone and the wines are capable of considerable elegance.

Il Poggione
Frazione Sant'Angelo in Colle, 53020 Montalcino SI. Tel 0577/864029; fax 0577/864165.
⊘🌢🍷 pp.62, 63
When winemaker here during the 1970s and 80s, Pierluigi Talenti made his own name and that of the estate, and he still consults here. The wines are consistent and long-lived. The Brunello is expensive; Rosso di Montalcino, concentrated and structured, offers the best value.

Poggio Scalette
Loc. Rùffoli, 50022 Greve in Chianti FI. Tel 055/8549017; fax 055/8547960. ⊘🌢 pp.8, 29, 41
Enologist Vittorio Fiore's own estate. Some very old vines have been discovered and have been added to new plantings of Sangiovese; Il Carbonaione is the stunning result.

Poliziano
Via Fontago 11, frazione Gracciano, 53040 Montepulciano SI. Tel & fax 0578/738171. ⊘🌢🍷 pp.67, 69, 71
Federico Carletti's dynamism and professionalism together with the best advice – lately

from Carlo Ferrini – has created wines that help lift the reputation of this zone. Besides the Vino Nobile (particularly Riservas Asinone and Caggiole), barrique-aged Elegia from Sangiovese and Le Stanze from Cabernet are notable. Decent Rosso and Vin Santo are also made.

Le Pupille
Loc. Pereta, 58051 Magliano in Toscana GR. Tel & fax 0564/505129. ⊘🌢🍷
Leading producer of Morellino di Scansano (Morellino is the local name for Sangiovese), a robust, scented red. The Riserva and Cabernet-dominant Saffredi are the most notable in a range of wines that have benefited from Giacomo Tachis' influence.

Querciabella
Via Santa Lucia Barbiano, Loc. Rùffoli, 50022 Greve in Chianti SI. Tel 055/853834; fax 055/8544657. ⊘🌢🍷 pp.8, 29, 41
Prestigious estate producing excellent Chianti Classico and Riserva and 2 remarkable super-Tuscans: the 80 per cent Sangiovese and 20 per cent Cabernet Camartina is powerful but beautifully made; the peerless Bâtard, from Pinot Bianco, Chardonnay and Pinot Grigio, is concentrated and classy.

Riecine
Loc. Riecine, 53013 Gaiole in Chianti SI. Tel & fax 0577/749527. ⊘🌢🍷 pp.32, 41
Much-praised estate owned by Englishman John Dunkley. The

well-structured, if initially austere, wines of real class and refinement are often outstanding. For Chianti Classico, Riserva and La Gioia, most of the grapes still come from high-altitude vineyards around the winery.

Rocca delle Macìe
Loc. Macìe, 53011 Castellina in Chianti SI. Tel 0577/743220; fax 0577/743150. ⊘🌢 pp.34
Commercially important estate owned by film-maker Zingarelli. Super-Tuscans Ser Gioveto and Roccato are of most interest.

Ruffino
Via Aretina 42–44, 50065 Pontassieve FI. Tel 055/8368259; fax 055/8313677. ⊘🌢🍷 pp.23, 28, 34, 40, 41, 58, 69, 71
Large but respected producer, whose estates include Nozzole, source of impressive Cabernet Il Pareto and Chianti Classico, and Villa Zano and Santedame in the Classico zone. Riserva Ducale Oro is highly regarded. Other successes include Cabreo Il Borgo (Sangiovese-Cabernet), Cabreo La Pietra (Chardonnay), Libaio (Chardonnay with a little Pinot Grigio) and Nero del Tondo (Pinot Nero). Ruffino also manage Il Greppone Mazzi in Montalcino and Lodola Nuova in Montepulciano.

San Felice
Loc. San Felice, frazione San Gusmè, 53019 Castelnuovo Berardenga SI. Tel 0577/359087; fax 0577/359223. ⊘🌢🍷 pp.33, 40, 42, 59
Important both as a producer of quality wines and for its experimental work. The Riserva Poggio Rosso is the best of the Chianti Classicos, while Vigorello is a fine barrique-aged Sangiovese with a little Cabernet. Chardonnay and Vin Santo are also noteworthy. The Campogiovanni estate, in the south of Montalcino commune, produces excellent Brunello.

San Giusto a Rentennano
Loc. Monti in Chianti, 53010 Gaiole in Chianti SI. Tel 0577/747121; fax 0577/747109.
⊘🌢🍷 pp.9, 33, 41

A producer of powerful long-lived wines. Chianti Classico, Riserva and the outstanding barrique-aged Sangiovese Percarlo only reach their full expression with sufficient bottle age. The stunning, expensive Vin Santo is predominantly Malvasia.

Tenuta San Guido

Loc. Capanne 27, 57020 Bolgheri LI. Tel 0565/762003; fax 0565/762017. ⊗ ● pp.8, 50, 53
The source of Sassicaia, a single wine that effectively created a new premium wine zone. Now President of the Consorzio, owner Marchese Incisa della Rocchetta is committed to advancing the whole zone.

Michele Satta

Loc. Vigna al Cavaliere, 57022 Castagneto Carducci LI. Tel & fax 0565/763894. ⊘ ● ● ● pp.52, 53
So far Michele Satta has concentrated on Sangiovese, in Vigna al Cavaliere, but he also has plantings of Merlot, Cabernet and Syrah. Piastraia is a new, possibly unique, blend of all 4 red varieties. La Costa di Giulia is barrique-fermented Vermentino. Simpler Bolgheri Bianco and Rosato are also made.

Selvapiana

Via Selvapiana 3, 50068 Rufina FI. Tel 055/8369848; fax 055/8316840. ⊘ ● ● pp.20-1, 23
With Frescobaldi, one of the 2 leading estates in Rufina zone. The impetus given by winemaker Federico Masseti, added to the direction of owner Francesco Giuntini and guidance of consultant Franco Bernabei, has resulted in even higher quality. Chianti Rufina, Riserva, Cru Vigna Bucerchiale and the new Fornacce are exceptional. All require some age: the best will improve for a decade or more. The new Pomino, Fattoria di Petrognano, shows promise.

Sorbaiano

Loc. Sorbaiano, 56040 Montecatini Val di Cécina PI. Tel 0588/30243; fax 0577/43226. ⊘ ● ● pp.50, 53

Advice from consultant Vittorio Fiore ensures the Sangiovese-based Rosso delle Miniere is successful, even in difficult vintages such as 1992. Humbler Montescudaio Bianco and Rosso are supple and inviting.

Talenti

Loc. Pian di Conte, frazione Sant'Angelo in Colle, 53020 Montalcino SI. Tel 0577/864043; fax 0577/864165. ⊘ ● pp.59, 62, 63
Pierluigi Talenti's own wines come from Pian di Conte, near Il Poggione, the estate which made his name. The Brunello, Riserva and Rosso are all excellent.

Tenuta del Terriccio

Via Bagnoli, loc. Le Badie, 56100 Castellina Marittima PI. Tel 050/699709; fax 050/699789. ⊘ ● ● pp.50, 53
A new star from the coast. Prices for the top Cabernet-Merlot Lupicaia, have rocketed, but since 1993 quality has also been high. More affordable are the Bordeaux-blend Tassinaie and the whites Rondinaia and Con Vento, a varietal Sauvignon.

Teruzzi & Puthod

Loc. Casale 19, 53037 San Gimignano SI. Tel 0577/940143; fax 0577/942016. ⊘ ● ● pp.46, 49
One wine has made the Ponte a Rondolino estate famous: Terre di Tufi, a refined barrique-aged Vernaccia. At least as good is the multi-variety Carmen, a fuller, stylish white. Peperino is a tasty Sangiovese-based red and there is a good sparkling wine, Sarpinello Brut.

Trerose

Via della Stella 3, frazione Valiano, 53040 Montepulciano SI. Tel 0578/724018; fax 02/90969365. ⊘ ● ● pp.68, 71
Former owner Lionello Marchesi continues to advise one

of Montepulciano's most modern estates. Several Vino Nobiles are produced, all with at least some aging in barrique. Whites include good Chardonnay (Salterio), Sauvignon (Flauto), Viognier (Liuto) and Vin Santo.

Tua Rita

Loc. Notri 81, 57028 Suvereto LI. Tel 0565/829237. ⊘ ● ● pp.52, 53
One of the stars of the little-known area around Suvereto, south of Bolgheri. Rita Tua and her husband, with consultant Luca d'Attoma, produce Giusto di Notri, an excellent Cabernet-Merlot blend. There is a tiny quantity of outstanding Merlot, as well as a number of other good wines, particularly whites.

Val di Suga

Loc. Val di Cava, 53024 Montalcino SI. Tel 0577/848701; fax 0577/849316. ⊘ ● pp.56, 62, 63
Part of the same group as Trerose. Investment in the vineyards and winery is expected to improve its current reputation. Most notable are the single-vineyard Brunellos (Vigna del Lago and Vigna Spuntali).

Valtellina

Loc. Rietine, 53013 Gaiole in Chianti SI. Tel 0577/731005; fax 0577/731083. ⊘ ● ● pp.8, 41
Outstanding small estate first made famous by Giorgio Regni, but continuing its rise under Christoph Schneider. Releases in the 1990s of Chianti Classico, Riserva and Sangiovese-Cabernet super-Tuscan Convivio have been superb.

Vecchie Terre di Montefili

Via San Cresci 47, 50022 Greve in Chianti FI. Tel 055/853739; fax 055/8544684 ⊘ ● ● pp.28, 41
Source of fabled super-Tuscans Anfiteatro (Sangiovese) and Bruno di Rocca (Cabernet with 30 per cent Sangiovese). There is also excellent Chianti Classico and, most recently, a fine white, Vigna Regis, a barrique-aged Chardonnay topped up with Sauvignon and Traminer.

Index of Other Wine Producers

For Main Wine Producers see pages 72–79.

Picture Credits
All photographs supplied by Cephas Picture Library (photographer Mick Rock) except for pp13 and 38 by Adrian Webster.

Author's Acknowledgments
Giampaolo Pacini, Donatella Cinelli-Colombini, Paolo Valdastri, Angelica Fagiuoli, Chaira Barioffi, Maddalena Mazzeschi, Caterina Dei, Marie-Sylvie and Roberto Melosi, Dr Francesco Giuntini, Marchese Bernardo Gondi, Marchese Leonardo de'Frescobaldi, Carlo Cioni, the Barsi family, Kim, Guy and Bella Millon.

Publisher's Acknowledgments
Guide: Trevor Lawrence (map illustrations), Aziz Khan (grape artworks), Steven Marwood (bottle photography).
Fold-out Map: Maurizio Castelli for help with the Chianti Classico, Brunello and Bolgheri panoramic maps, and Paolo Solini at the Consorzio del Vino Nobile di Montepulciano for help with the Montepulciano panoramic map.